Vaugh Rapatahana

More than the Existentialist Outsider:

Reflections on the work of
Colin Wilson

❀

[Colin Wilson Studies # 29]

Paupers' Press

Colin Wilson Studies # 29
Series editor: Colin Stanley

Published by:
Paupers' Press,
37 Quayside Close,
Turney's Quay,
Nottingham NG2 3BP
England.

Printed and bound in the UK by KnowledgePoint
Limited, Reading.

ISBN: 978-0-9955978-3-9

www.pauperspress.co.uk
For our complete catalogue of books, see our website or write to the
above address or e-mail us at: **stan2727uk@aol.com**

Contents

A Personal Foreword

[From the PhD thesis 1995]

❀

When I was a teenage youth, trying hard to grow my hair as long as those other hippie heroes back in the late sixties, I was living in a caravan on the back lawn of my parents' place in South Auckland—with my umbilical cord as the electrical lead stretching across into the power point embedded in their lounge wall. I was a seventh former and my brains were only just starting to gel into any substantive form (they still haven't reached their zenith as I type nearly twenty-five years later). One thing is for sure, I felt alienated from just about everything and only found solace in listening to Jim Morrison and Steppenwolf and, occasionally, in the arms of blonde fourth form farm girls who wrote that they loved me in ballpoint pen on their arms and wrists.

So when David Eggleton banged on the door of my thin skinned caravan one day clutching a paperback book and saying: "Have you seen this?" I took note of the title and the strange cover where one profile was distanced from the others. Eggleton was fired by *The Outsider* and soon so was I. Even while reading the book I too felt that I was an Outsider—in fact knew it down to the very depths of my soul. I too felt the "nausea" rankling in my bones and my gut—it was quite literally a physical presence. I too thought almost everyone else was a fuckwit, I too could not understand why no one else seemed even remotely concerned about why they were alive. I mean, why the hell were we all obsessed with Vietnam and rugby union? Why was my old man drinking himself to death every night down at the 'Cosi' Club? Why did idiots like Holyoake have so much credence? What was the meaning of life?

I guess Colin Wilson's portentous book articulated my incompatibility with Mother Life; and it articulated my dread, the complete schism that separated the Outsider from what it seemed everyone else was doing. *The Outsider* was then, and remains now, a bible for disturbed youth.

I went on a Colin Wilson reading binge over the next few months. I borrowed Campion's premature biography from the Papatoetoe library and scoured second hand bookshops, like a character from a Wilson novel, for other works. By this time I was a freshman—literally—at the University of Auckland and was discovering a whole new world—philosophy, especially Existentialism. Clive Pearson and Bernie Pflaum were splendid lightbulbs in the mist of the academic smoke screen that was logical positivism and Rylean apoplexy. Everyone else seemed to be B-grade actors in a William Beaudine movie, I struggled up and down the creaking stairs of the old clock tower to hear Pearson's tirades against politicians and most other members of the rest of the department. Still, I could never understand why Colin Wilson was never mentioned—a man who was continuously querying the whyfores and wherefores of human existence, and whose *Religion and the Rebel* in its 1957 version I had gobbled up in the University Bookshop one afternoon. Wilson was an Existentialist, what is more he was a new type of Existentialist—refining the estrangement that is the birth pang of the Outsider into a new cluster of ideas about evolution. Why did no one else share my interest?

A Personal Foreword

I continued at University—dropping too much acid, drinking too much beer at the Kiwi, noting James K. Baxter over in the corner, and still very much an apostle of Wilson. As I sped through *Beyond the Outsider* I wanted to shout: "This guy is saying something important, why don't you listen?" I felt that I was in a cavernous room and that everyone else was wacked out on Mandrax and moving so damnably slow that they could not keep up with what I was saying about Wilson—many were in fact asleep or at best merely propping one another up to keep from collapsing into unmanageable shapes on the floor, making no real effort to listen to me. (In fact I distinctly remember being at such a party in Onehunga—but that is another story.)

Wilson remained a mentor figure for years and I continued to read his latest works as avidly as I could, although I confess to disappointment when he became—to me anyway—a kind of New Age guru in the 1970s. I once wrote to him and said this, and he kindly replied that he felt no inconsistency between his early work and his later occult springboard leaps—that everything was an extension of his fundamental vision, that Man was more than he let on to himself. I guessed that he was right, but being young I wanted an answer to the meaning of life immediately, and all this stuff about Uri Geller and poltergeists—while very entertaining—seemed to me a distraction. Wilson obviously was engaged in diversionary tactics while he prepared the incipient BIG statement. I didn't want to think that he did not have the secret password, or worse still, had sold out to Captain Megabucks, the scourge of the Western World.

Yet one thing is certain—Wilson acted as a young man's guide to the galaxy. He listed so many names and books and historical episodes that I was constantly learning about all sorts of subjects that I would have never encountered had I not read his books. In those days every Wilson philosophical work was a magic lantern of learning. I found myself nodding in agreement or saying "right on"—as we so stupidly did back then.

Over in the English Department where I was a vague chela, I tried to lay the basics of Existential Literary Criticism on largely unhearing ears. Only Roger Horrocks had the decency at least to listen to what I felt was so manifestly the way to judge literature—not by analysing iambic pentameter or metaphysical conceits or objective correlatives or seven kinds of ambiguity.

The 1970s rolled on. I had always meant to 'do' a PhD in philosophy—something to do with somehow solidifying the liquid that is identity, or with my formulation of The Doctrine of Ultimate Pointlessness which stipulated no basic rationale for life even if there were meanings. But events got in the way. I was by now married with two preschool children. I was a secondary schoolteacher—which felt like being a zookeeper armed with one banana in a cage full of hungry chimpanzees. Colin Wilson was still a hero but I was increasingly distracted by trying pragmatically to make ends meet—a problem the newly married Wilson himself had, and made clear in his autobiographical writings. I still felt 'on the outside,' so to speak, but there was not the sense of abrasiveness or the inner gnawing as in those angst-filled years of my late teens. I began to wonder if in fact outsiderism was really only a neurotic affliction. I started to think about colour TVs and mortgages. I even found myself mowing the lawn—with a motor mower too.

Yet Wilson still had a hold on me—even if his books seemed to have lost the dagger thrust of his early metaphysical masterpieces. I would find things like *L'Amour* in the sex section of second hand book shops and laugh, musing that good old Wilson never let an opportunity to make a buck slide by, and I would return the book to the shelf.

I began to believe that I was a detainee in some sort of karass with the man when one day, whilst getting dental treatment from Frank Copeland, a Maughamian alcoholic on the island of Nauru, while watching the geckos skirt the dowdy plaster on the ceiling of his humid surgery, we for some obscure reason began to talk about Colin Wilson. Copeland told me that he had been Wilson's next door neighbour in Cornwall for years and knew him well. Here I was in Godforsakenland with Wilson's neighbour, whose febrile dentist's hands were nearing my mouth with ganglionated fingers. It obviously wasn't enough that my birthday was on the same day as Wilson's. Maybe there was something in all of his occult palaver after all.

Life went on. The marriage broke up. My father died in my arms at the age of 48. I went mad and was put away for a while with the inmates of Stirling Villa, way up the top of the hill, miles from 'normality', socialising with them a lot better than I had with most people outside of the institution. There were suicide attempts, intrusions into taha Maori, new relation-ships, wanderlust, moronic interludes in massage parlours, jobs in Mt Wellington steelyards driving fork lifts with 'the boys', until I began to realise that the hippies were dead, and so was macho New Zealand sexist masculinity, and my life was a merry go round and the painted horses made no sense. I wrote my head off in a motorbike smash and stopped drinking and smoking dope for good. I grew up overnight.

The vision of actually 'doing' a PhD on Wilson sustained me and I nagged academics silly until they finally admitted me to the bar of study. I kept reading Wilson, although without the messianistic zeal of my youth. I still felt he had something vital to say—even if it was somewhat dissipated by the smog fumes of the paranormal. I admired the man for not relenting in his quest for the meaning of life, for constantly setting out on his ambitious expeditions while most others sat at home watching television.

I kept running into people that knew him, and on one occasion into someone who lived half a mile away from me— Les Watkins—who had 'been' Wilson for a period while the writer was recovering from panic attacks. Les even had some books owned by Wilson and borrowed from him years before, with Wilson's name-stamp embossed inside them, which I ended up posting back to Gorran Haven. Synchronicity or merely coincidence? Fate seemed to be beckoning—do this thesis, do it now!

I became exasperated with reading the same anecdotes about Proust dipping biscuits into tea; about Graham Greene playing Russian Roulette with a loaded revolver; about humans being like grandfather clocks driven by watch-springs—but then I remembered that this was a writer who had had to make a living, and half of his gigantic sandwich spread of volumes can be excused for that reason. As for my thesis, it became a serious attempt to consider Wilson in his own terms, and to argue that despite his many failings he remained worthy of study, that the problems he continuously worried about were of fundamental importance, and that it was time we all started to take him a little more seriously as a novelist, a philosopher, a critic, and above all, a visionary mystic. He has outlasted most of his peers and judges, he hasn't backed away from the challenge he set himself, he—

even now—opens up interesting new perspectives as we read him.

So the man is still part of my life, and I still want to chisel a little of his insight into the collective dead wood of our culture. To conclude this personal foreword, let me become even more metaphorical. Imagine I was about to hitch-hike to Wellington one hot summer holiday a quarter of a century ago when an Englishman—whose name I later learnt was Wilson—picked me up in his droll motorcar. I threw my bag onto the backseat which was covered in dozens of books—no, actually it was hundreds—and we set off down the highway— with some classical music on the radio (Wilson was humming along with it). Twenty five years later we are still on our way to Wellington. We went off the road years ago, broke down a couple of times, had several near misses. Other travellers have jumped inside for a while then vanished *en route*, oddballs with names like Jaynes and Lethbridge and Lovecraft. There was Crowley too—and that German, Friedrich something or other, a great talker. Many times I have been tempted to say to Wilson, the driver of this fuelless Dinky toy "Let me out here!" In fact, I have sometimes reached over to grab my delicately balanced bag from the back seat and slammed my hand onto the door handle ready to spring out—but here I am still riding in the car, somewhere in the universe. I know that we will never reach Wellington, but it has ceased to matter. Wilson will never turn the car round and head back to anywhere as mundane as that. But I'm not getting out until the end.

The Colin Wilson Interview, September, 1993.

Introduction

I was nearing completion of my PhD thesis at the University of Auckland, New Zealand. The title was *Existential Literary Criticism and the Novels of Colin Wilson*. Ideally, it would have been great to actually meet the man and to talk with him, rather than receive letters from afar.

I wrote rather extensively about why I had come to this study at the beginning of the thesis, as finally completed in 1996 (see Addendum One here). One significant factor was a certain synchronicity, almost as if I was being directed to write about Wilson; such were the coincidences and fortunate signs steering my pathway, ever since I first read *The Outsider* in 1969.

In 1993 Wilson was invited as a guest at the Melbourne Writers Festival in Australia. I seized the opportunity to fly to Melbourne forthwith after I learned of his impending appearance from Howard Dossor in a letter from January that year. He had been of immense help supplying resources and patiently answering my manifold questions during the course of writing the thesis and we had kept up a continual correspondence (before email) which continues to this day (via emails). Dossor, of course, had extensive meetings and correspondence with Wilson and had travelled to Gorran Haven no less than eleven times already. It was Dossor who arranged separate lectures by Wilson, during this 1993 visit.

Colin Wilson Interview

Colin Wilson and I also had a chain of communication stretching back to 1985; again via so-called 'snail mail' in the earlier stages. Once I knew he was going to come to Melbourne, I wrote to him and asked if he would be able to make it to Auckland, New Zealand. He replied via postcard, that no he could not make it this time. All the more incentive for me to organise travel and accommodation in Australia.

It was one of the latter separate lectures, which Dossor titled *A Creative Consciousness*, that I attended. The crowd was large and intent. The lecture was well-received and cogent, as Wilson was in fine form. He spoke clearly and articulately, as well as fielded several questions from interested audience members at the conclusion of his lecture. I was impressed by the manner of his delivery, his careful description of significant terms, his overall enthusiasm.

Howard Dossor had also issued an invitation to me to attend an after-seminar meeting with Colin Wilson, which is where this interview took place, over bottles of fine red wine. I found Colin, once again, extremely affable and generous with his time, whilst his responses were concise but full of detail. Dossor and Joy Wilson were also in attendance, so the occasion was sociable, relaxed and convivial. They were very patient, for Wilson and I spoke for some considerable time.

I mentioned that I would be flying back to Auckland the next day and Wilson told me that they would also be transiting there, before going on to the States. We were not on the same aeroplane, it seems, although he did look around for me, as he wrote in an email afterwards. I also recall seeking him on the plane, to the extent of asking cabin crew if he was on board, which they could not confirm. I later figured that he was transiting in New Zealand *en route* to San Francisco, I believe, and that in fact we took completely different flights at around the same time. It seems synchronicity was off duty at that time!

Colin Wilson in Melbourne, September 1993

Prologue:
Getting to Meet the Man

I finally got around to meeting Colin Wilson in September 1993. He was to be a participant in the Melbourne Writer's Festival. Howard Dossor had informed me of this months before and I set my sights on travelling to Australia to meet with the subject of this thesis. I had to scrimp and save and place myself further into impecuniosity to attain the airfare; but I was determined to get there.

Dossor also kindly arranged for Wilson to be interviewed by me, so armed with my Kambrook tape recorder, I went up to the Footscray campus of the Victoria University of Technology to be introduced to, and to question Colin Wilson.

Colin was a portly gentleman; most noticeable because of his distinctive checkered floppy hat which made him look like he was out on a fishing expedition. I found him to be amiable, amenable and relaxed. He was a little unwell after contacting some airborne bacteria on the aeroplane over and was very obviously tired. But he generously gave his time, and over a bottle of wine, settled down to answer in some considerable detail my questions specifically about Existential Literary Criticism and his own novels. I reproduce in full the text of that 'interview' at the end of this thesis. We tended to go away from this subject quite often—for example we ended up talking about Marilyn Monroe—but we also had quite a few laughs. There was a sense of Wilson having his answers a little off pat—he had obviously been through this routine many times before. But he was not just going through the motions, he warmed to the task, and it seemed a productive session all round.

Later I sat in a front row seat—again the work of the generous Howard Dossor, a man who will not condone any attempts to diminish Wilson—at an address called 'Colin Wilson discusses Consciousness Unbounded'. Wilson certainly appears to believe deeply everything that he is saying. He is an inspiring speaker, who gives the occasional droll comment, and the occasional deliberately stirring remark like: "I'm almost a fascist", but who can stimulate the audience. The full house listened intently and question time was unfortunately cut short before it could last all night: one felt Wilson would have replied to all the upcoming interrogations. Wilson has the knack of getting the individual to nod in agreement: 'Yes', one feels, 'I've had that sort of experience. I know what he is saying'. The relational consciousness starts to expand exponentially, the grasping for 'higher' levels of consciousness begins in earnest. I noted even the Chancellor afterwards speaking as an inspired man, he too had been touched by the sheer positivity of Wilson's message and delivery.

Afterwards at dinner Wilson was quiet, his tiredness obvious. He offered at his own behest to make notes on this very thesis—after his return from his impending tour to the States. (I decided, however, not to take up this offer before the thesis was marked.) His visit to Melbourne had gone well— he earned his money, he established audience rapport, he ended up autographing dozens of proffered books. The pity is that he has not ever been formally invited to New Zealand. He could—on reflection—make a mint out of touring as a kind of 'Power of Positive Thinking' guru. But he is still very much bound up in writing. As later noted, he regards his still-to-be-completed sequel to *The Space Vampires* "the best I have ever written".

It was my judgement that he threw out no new ideas or information, that he said nothing to upset the thrust of this thesis. My lasting impression is that he is the 'proverbial good chap' who is strong and settled in his beliefs, his ambitions, his place in the world. When the positive philosophy he espouses eventually becomes a commonplace he feels that he will become "the patron saint of the...movement". Whether or not he ever acquires guru status he deserves at least to be taken a good deal more seriously than he is at present. He has stuck to his mission steadfastly for over forty years now, never wavering from what he sees as his job'. He deserves more attention both as writer and as mystic.

I have left my transcript of the interview largely unedited. My intent was completeness, rather than fluidity. I felt that our conversation should be presented exactly as it happened.

A Conversation between Colin Wilson and Vaughan Rapatahana,

held at Footscray Campus,
Victoria University of Technology, Melbourne, Australia,
September 16, 1993

VR: In your later publications...I can find no reference to Existential Literary Criticism *per se* and I wondered why this may be. I mean there seems to be no real allusion to the theory anymore. Are there any reasons for this? Is it still of total relevance to you in 1993?

CW: Oh it's of relevance to me all right, but don't forget this sort of theory of mine developed in this period about thirty years ago, when literary criticism was...I mean the era of T.S. Eliot and Leavis was just coming to an end but literary criticism was still very, very fuddy-duddy and even then the emphasis was all on the text and the meaning of the text, and of course I'd always taken T.E. Hulme's comment very much to heart...that don't look at the philosophy, look at the philosopher, and in that sense it's not that it has become less relevant since then, it's simply that in the kind of work I've been doing since then, particularly in the paranormal and so on, in criminology, and it's no longer relevant in the way that it was in the days I was writing about literary criticism.

VR: Which leads onto the next question. Ever since *The Occult* back in '71 which changed your material life obviously, because you've made that clear in several interviews, you don't seem to write so much straight what we'd call philosophy or straight literary criticism...

CW: Well I don't know. As I say in that book *Beyond The Occult* I made a real attempt to summarise everything, the whole lot—*The Outsider* and so on. I also tried to do it in *Mysteries*. Because I've got a feeling that all my work in a sense is part of the same big circle. I mean I noticed that even last night I began talking in Sydney about crime because they had put me down to talk about crime for some strange reason. I started off by briefly talking about Romanticism in the nineteenth century and all that sort of thing, then I went into crime and long before the end of the evening talking about people like Ted Bundy and so on, we'd got around to the beginning of the evening again, so to speak, we'd come up with a circle and they could see the connection between my ideas on crime and existentialism, mysticism, romanticism and so on.

VR: I see the connection right through. There's that logical strand going right through. But the actual...I call it 'ELT' because I can't be bothered writing it Existential Literary Theory all the time...you don't refer to it specifically. I know it's of relevance to you. I know that everything you write is coming from that perspective...but no sort of Colin Wilson writing about ELT.

CW: Well I suppose...and don't forget also I don't write a great deal of literary criticism...

VR: No, you don't.

CW: I write things for the *Literary Review* and...but you know it doesn't really arise...

VR: You used to though. Used to do a lot of that. You wrote books like *The Strength to Dream* and compilation *Eagle and Earwig* etcetera. I would personally like to see more of that sort of thing because I'm basically a philosopher at heart you see. To me your most important book was *Introduction to the New Existentialism*. I understand all the other, later strands of that but I look at it from a philosophical perspective: very much anti-analytic, anti-Logical Positivist...

CW: Absolutely.

VR: who still today, especially in New Zealand, dominate and decimate the universities. It's like talking to that wall...

CW: Oh, yeah.

VR: They do...I did my...as I said to Howard earlier today...I did my Masters about twenty odd years ago in Existential Philosophy, in New Zealand. It was hard, almost impossible. I was fighting pitched battles with these morons who wanted to go on about sense data; was that a sense data or a chair? All this sort of crap. But you know that. OK, which leads on to my next question. About the same time as *The Occult* came out you sort of dissipated the number of novels you wrote *per se*. Before there was a sort of, not quite annual, but a fairly constant supply of novels. Was there any particular reason for that sort of slowing down?

CW: Ah let me think...I can't remember which novels I've written since *The Occult* came out. *The Personality Surgeon*...

and it never happened with philosophical works like *The Outsider* and so this is what began to fascinate me with novels, and then once again with *Adrift in Soho*, my second novel. I mean it began to take shape and of course a big chunk of that is actually based on a play—*The Metal Flower Blossom*, but...I began to enjoy it so much, writing it simply because the play solidified—it turned into real people and events. Now that has always fascinated me.

VR: The novel is writing you, you're not writing the novel

CW: That's exactly what it is, and the same thing happened with this *Metamorphosis of the Vampire*.

VR: How much, how much do you use a novel—and I think you probably do use it—to think? I know that when I write novels I use them to think, to get rid of a lot of stuff, like you just said, that I wasn't even conscious of—even consciously happening—but when I wrote it down, it came out, it was actually quite good. How much do you do that? I mean you've admitted to doing that a couple of times.

CW: Well I don't use the novel exactly to think. I tend to think as it were in flashes and spurts, that is I suddenly get an insight and develop the insight and there's not really room to do this in a novel. A novel as I say is not concerned with thinking, it's concerned with creating solid situations which seem to solidify of themselves. I don't know if you've ever done this but when you're dreaming sometimes or on the edge of sleep you find that you can actually see things...you can actually look at a scene which you know is in your head and it looks quite solid. Now this is what comes with a novel.

VR: Yes. So to me a novel is cathartic. I don't know if you feel the same thing. Very cathartic. Which leads onto another point...which you've also said many times. How much is novel writing really a financial thing; you've had to write to survive economically? In the early days anyway?

CW: Oh I still do to some extent. But no, novel writing was never a financial thing in that sense.

VR: It wasn't that necessary?

CW: Oh no, because in point of fact I don't think my novels ever made any more money than my non-fiction books. See my work has never made a lot of money. If you're writing about ideas you don't make money. What does happen of course and what has happened over the years very, very slowly is that you suddenly discover that you've got a big enough audience with a few pence trickling in from all over the world to just about keep you happy. So...you meet people in Melbourne who know all kinds of things about your work that amaze you and you realise you've got an audience.

(At this stage, I get up and show Colin the first issue of *Quote Unquote*, a New Zealand magazine.)

VR: That's a New Zealand publication. The ten most stolen books ....in alphabetical order.

CW: I'm glad I'm the tenth.

VR: That shows...It's not...ranked numerically. It's ranked in alphabetical order. You're not tenth at all. You're just any one of those ten.

CW: Oh, I see. I see.

VR: It's not a ranking scale of who is the most stolen. You are one of the most stolen authors in one of the main bookshops throughout the country in New Zealand. Which leads back to what you say—there's a sort of clique of Colin Wilson. As I said to Howard, when I wanted to get some Colin Wilson books on Interloan, like *The Geller Phenomenon*, they didn't have it in Auckland Library—they had to get it up from Dunedin. They wouldn't let me do that because it was an 'occult' book and it would go missing—because it was written by you.

CW: Oh yes, some girl last night got me to sign a library copy of *Encyclopaedia of Murder* and I said: You know it will just go missing now.

VR: You just get ripped off all the time by these people, don't you?

(At this stage Colin stood up to blow his nose, talking about the 'change of climate and antibiotics and germs picked up on the plane in the air conditioning system...')

VR: You'll have to write a novel about these bacteria...You claim, especially in *The Craft of The Novel* and also in the Introduction to *The Mind Parasites*, the Sauk City one, that the novel should be as much entertainment as it is sort of didacticism. How much do you reckon you've achieved entertainment value—that's a big enough word—in your novels?

CW: I'd have thought sort of...up to a fairly high level. You see I've always aimed to write something people will want to keep on reading. I've never really liked these kind of novelists who spend a chapter and a half telling you about their characters and so on and their history before they get into the novel so you're forced to make this terrific act of faith, sort of like those mystery bus tours, you're forced to...or they describe in enormous detail a plane coming into land in Hong Kong and the bloke going through the customs and so on, and twenty pages later the stories are gradually getting started. With all my novels, I've had this desire to get started with the first sentence and into it.

VR: How much do you feel your novels are didactic? To me many of them, not all of them, are fairly didactic.

CW: Oh I would have thought, I mean they're all novels of ideas. I mean I would have said that I'm primarily and basically a novelist of ideas...

VR: You do say that.

CW: I'm very much like someone like Ayn Rand who's probably the last major novelist of ideas in the Twentieth Century. She irritates me very much, because she's so simplistic and crude.

VR: You got into a fair bit of, not hot water, but I can't remember the right cliche, but her supporters over in her office, over in the States...Didn't you?

CW: Oh you know what happened there don't you?

VR: You criticized her or they thought you criticized her.

CW: Barbara Brandon, the wife of Nathaniel Brandon, sent me her book finally, her biography of Ayn Rand, I think it's called *The Passion of Ayn Rand*, and there sort of on page 210 there's a long footnote saying about her husband Nathaniel and the way he acted as a sort of god, not allowing other people to approach the goddess and saying Colin Wilson in fact wrote to Ayn Rand two or three times and got a very dusty answer back from Nathaniel. Now the funny thing was that by this time Nathaniel had already written to me, had already broken with Ayn Rand, sending me his books and only a few weeks ago his latest book on psychology came in proof and I...said some nice things about him which he's going to put on the cover and shall probably see him this time on the West Coast of America. So it's funny, all things come round in cycles sooner or later.

VR: They do. It's all back to synchronicity like you said. Howard and I talked about them. (At this stage we had a long digression about Frank Copeland, Wilson's ex-next door neighbour in Cornwall, whom I had met up with on Nauru. Most of the chat was me raving on about the weirdness of the place.)

VR: OK. The alienation effect—another term you used a lot in the early days, but again it doesn't seem to come to the fore anymore. Is it of relevance to you anymore?

CW: In what sense?

VR: Well do you still sort of aim at an alienation effect; that you're writing a sort of wink/nudge to the audience—saying don't take this too seriously, the actual ideas are what's important. Do you think you do that or...

CW: Well, no don't forget what I said, I think it was at the back of *Man Without a Shadow* wasn't it?

VR: No, it was at the back of *God of the Labyrinth*—and it was also an interview with Diana Cooper-Clark plus about nine other places, but we won't get all esoteric...

CW: What I was saying basically was simply that as far as I'm concerned the novel is a way of getting over ideas and that therefore in a certain sense there's always that wink and the nudge to the reader. I mean this latest book, I found as I said, *Metamorphosis of Vampire*, I began to develop this idea about the grandson of Carlsen in *The Space Vampires* and...the fact that he discovers he's a vampire, that he's inherited it from his grandfather and then he suddenly discovers New York is full of vampires, that these people are still left over and they're perfectly benevolent, wanting to simply suck energy from other people, never enough to damage them, until he discovers there's still sort of malevolent vampires around, that's the base of the plot but as soon as...of course the point of the book in a way is this notion of vampirism. The first time he meets this female vampire, sort of perfectly sweet girl—he meets her father, and the father says demonstrate to him, and she opens his flies and takes out his prick and puts her arms around his neck and pulls down her knickers far enough to be able to insert his prick just between her thighs which closes on it and then she puts her tongue in his mouth and suddenly he becomes aware of what is happening: there's this wonderful energy flowing from her tongue, going down to his prick, going through in her and going back up there and suddenly there's this perfect circuit and what's more there's no need for sort of sexual excitement. On one occasion where he does have an orgasm they sort of say 'Naughty, naughty, you're not supposed to do that'. What actually happens, he realises, is an interpenetration of the two personalities. He's left with a bit of her in him and she's left with a bit of him in her. And he suddenly thinks: 'My God, this is what sex is supposed to be'. We human beings with that sort of crude ramming of physical flesh into physical flesh is nothing to do with the essence of sex and...

VR: You write about that in *L'Amour* very well.

CW: Ah yes and I'd forgotten that until I saw a copy of it the other day.

VR: It's almost mystical actually. My main thrust in my thesis which...it's written, but I'm going to hone it now I've spoken to you, is that you're basically a Romantic.

CW: Oh of course I am...

VR: And a mystic

CW: I've never denied that I'm a Romantic.

31

Colin Wilson Interview

VR: I see Colin Wilson as a *prima facie* English Romantic...I'm quite serious.

CW: Well you know, I mean you know my work well enough to know my basic position which is I was fascinated by the Romantics, particularly by Goethe and Schiller when I was young and to a lesser extent by Wordsworth and Shelley—and particularly by Hoffman—that this fascination of the Romantics filled me with a kind of fizzy optimism...even Jean-Paul. You know if you'd been alive in 1810 and you'd asked anybody who is the greatest writer in the world they'd have said Shakespeare, Dante and Jean-Paul.

VR: No one knows who he is anymore...

CW: Absolutely.

VR: And Novalis—they think Novalis is a hair cream. No, I categorise you as a Positive Romantic.

CW: But then you see Romanticism seemed to fizzle out into depression. Now my feeling was very strongly there was something there that should not have been allowed to fizzle out, that should not have been allowed to escape. In other words you've got a kind of scent which nobody had ever bottled, which has been allowed to evaporate into the air and turn sour and I had this strong feeling that if you were just clever enough, if you were a great enough chemist, you could distil this scent and put a glass stopper in and it wouldn't evaporate and this is what all my novels are—an attempt to get this scent into the bottle.

VR: And it hasn't evaporated. You've still got that mission going. You are one of the Romantics that have remained alive and keeps on the tradition. Which is great...You are, fundamentally to me, basically a Romantic novelist and a mystic because some of your stuff tends to sort of mysticism.

CW: You can also see though that one of the most fundamental things about me is that I'm cheerful. I'm a cheerful type. That has always meant that I've never been able to sort of accept this modern notion of gloom and depression that permeates the whole of modern literature...

VR: And philosophy.

CW: Very much philosophy too of course. And of course this is partly just a sort of intellectual thing, that is the French tend to be the main exponents of modern philosophy are...basically negative...You've always got this idea behind Sartre, Camus and then more recently Foucault and Derrida, Roland Barthes...

VR: And their literary criticism which I don't fully understand quite frankly.

CW: Well, I quite agree with you.

VR: It's gobbledegook.

CW: Behind the gobbledegook, is in fact the feeling that you have no essential *you* inside you—it's merely a collection of impressions and so on just as David Hume says, and secondly that these moments in which you have a feeling of sudden meaning which Derrida calls presence, are once again illusion in that he says they are constituted effects. It's not a sudden glimpse of essence, of truth, and of course this completely negative view is a view that has got to be overturned. Now whether it will happen in my lifetime I don't know. What I do feel that is when it does happen I shall be regarded as a patron saint of the movement.

VR: I hope so, because you are one of the few people out there actually doing it, I mean the sort of optimistic side.

CW: Yes, it's taken such a long time. I mean I'm 62 now you know and it...nevertheless it does seem to be happening. You suddenly realise something is happening, people are getting interested.

VR: People are still stealing your books. That leads onto only a couple more questions. I know you're busy and tired. How much scope do you sort of give to the unconscious? The will, the individual will, the person with the ability to do something, not necessarily the dominant 5%, the person who is slightly ahead, outside, who's got a sort of individual willpower to do something is your main man. But how do you sort of ascribe to unconscious...sort of motivations, things a person has no control over himself? Do you see sort of any area for that sort of...

(Note: In the next section of the interview I was trying to articulate an area of concern that I have made only piecemeal reference to throughout this thesis: that is the overall role of the sub/unconscious. Wilson acknowledges its presence—as for example in his assignation of occult faculties as reposing there—but he wants to say that the intentionally conscious I/the Transcendental Ego, is the pilot of the ship. I'm by no means so certain that sheer conscious willpower and positivity can refute any potential and pre-determined dark denizens from the deep. And, as Paul Newman, from Tim Dalgleish, further complicates: "Dalgleish sees Wilson's philosophy as an active contradiction, in that he (Wilson) allows the mind a subconscious stratum, yet also allows freewill" (a). Just how does the free will fit in with the predetermined?

More, I'm also not so certain that these two self-same voluntary agencies, willpower and positivity, can ensure peak experiences and the entire upper echelons of the Wilsonian mystic spectrum, all of which are themselves the issues of an amalgamatory act; all stemming from the whole mind. I wonder just how much the mind is influenced by purely physiologic forces, and I try to express this in the following questions. For as Newman, *qua* Dalgleish, again proffers: "Tim Dalgleish expresses...the epiphenomenal nature of the peak experience" (b).)

((a) Paul Newman, review of *The Guerilla Philosopher*, Tim Dalgleish, Abraxas 6, St Austell Cornwall, 1994, pp 22/23 (b). ibid p 23.)

CW: Well now you see, you must have noticed that in my work my feeling about the unconscious tends to be quite positive. The unconscious on the whole is a good source, a source that works for good. The unconscious is what wakes you up in the morning when you know you've got to be awake at five o'clock.

Colin Wilson Interview

VR: I realise that—you go into right/left brain sort of sides it's the same sort of thing, but I'm talking about unconscious, areas that a person has no control over, wasn't even aware of, sort of suppressed sort of memories and things like that...but that area has never come out in your work.

CW: As you know I've always been such an anti-Freudian and always felt...that Freud was completely negative and that this was a mistake on his part.

VR: Are you saying there's no suppressed sort of areas, areas out of a person's control?

CW: What I am saying, I think, is that your own conscious negativity often exaggerates and amplifies those repressed areas...when in fact...it would be fairly easy to have them flow out in some natural way.

VR: Some people have got repressed areas they're not even aware of, that sort of motivate them to be people they're not really at all.

CW: No, there's an idea that I'll put forward this evening if I have got time—you can never tell what you're going to say— and that is that there are three distinct levels of control in human beings, and you can talk about the first level of control, which happens when you are tired or when you are just in an ordinary state of consciousness, you feel on the whole that your body is more or less conditioned to do certain things and there's not a great deal you can do about this, you feel that circumstances move you along.

Now when you move up to the second level of control...it's like going into second gear in your car. Quite suddenly, you get this odd feeling of strength and power and you get this odd feeling that you are much more in control than you realise. In the third level of control happiness, excitement, the racing driver going 110 miles an hour. Quite suddenly, you know that you are in control...

VR: We need to do this permanently. All I'm saying, Colin is that back in the first level are some areas that you haven't got any access to, you weren't even aware existed at all—that sort of make you what you are.

CW: Well I've never experienced this myself.

VR: I have...I had to have hypnotherapy to find certain suppressed areas that I didn't know even existed. Until they were out of my system I wasn't really functioning 100%—so that's an area that's important to me, that's a personal experience. I had hypnotherapy, it clarified, like one of those comic lightbulbs you see when a light bulb goes on inside someone's head, and it thinks, 'Ah, that's what it's all about'. That happened to me, and suddenly—I didn't transform but it clarified a lot of subconscious crap up, that had been driving me, impelling me, wasn't even aware of; suppressed memories of something quite nasty. You see, what I'm trying to say is that certain areas of human consciousness the human individual doesn't know themselves. I was transformed—that anxiety, that neurotic side of me, just dissipated—I became a happy chappy permanently. So, this was an area in me that I didn't really know, was impelling me, making me a person I really wasn't. That's the area I'm trying to ask you about, you don't really ever cover that. To me there are certain areas in people who've you've called neurotics and psychotics who are like that but they don't know why they're like that. So, that's a personal experience, that happened.

CW: No, I'm absolutely certain that this is so, but...it's not a thing I've had any experience of, and also as you can see I tend to be a little like Ramakrishna—the belief when he says you know though a man may be the greatest of sinners this knowledge will carry him like a raft above his sin. I also tend to believe that although I can quite see an important way of discovering...what is holding you back would be hypnotherapy or whatever...a second way would be simply if you were carried away so much by what you were doing, for example writing a novel or something of the sort, it would be possible as it were to go into racing driver gear.

VR: Those puerile poems I sent you all those years ago were impelled by that experience, but I didn't know that. It wasn't until I had the hypnotherapy and it sort of all clicked and I could move into about nineteenth gear, which I am most of the time; but I was going into reverse all of the time—so that's an interesting thing—which leads onto the last couple of questions. How much of your theory is a sort of account of physiology, sort of the actual brain chemistry where the will has no real control, where...(you) just might have too much to drink, a person might take drugs or something and their whole physiological system can be transformed? How do you see that area, you know what I mean? Or all these new sort of...brain permutations and things now. How much can an individual say I will force myself to attempt to get 'there' and how much can it be done, I guess, by artificial means? I don't know.

CW: I don't know. I'm sure it can be done by artificial means. There are all these artificial...I nevertheless feel that...Tim Leary once said that what interested him about psychedelics...was the question of how you could re-induce the state once you'd learnt to get there without the psychedelics...that seemed to be the really interesting thing. Now as far as I can see the most basic thing about that is a certain feeling of as it were optimism, the feeling that everything is OK. A real problem is that once we begin to get tired, and physically low, this is the time when all of your neuroses, all of your problems leap up from your unconscious mind and sit on your head. Once you actually succeed in getting rid of these, to a large extent, things like tiredness and you know sort of nasty shocks, they still have a certain amount of impact but it's not that exaggerated and amplified by your own problems. So you know as you can see, I basically tend to take a rather optimistic point of view.

VR: Yes, I just see the other side.

CW: No. I do see it.

VR: Well all the optimism would not prevail, where certain people are so stuffed in the head literally, to use an old cliché, that all the optimism in the world is not going to help them, they're fighting something that has gone on for years before or they're fighting physiological deformities and things like that. That's an area...Last question. Style in the novels; back to the novels. How much scope or attention do you really give to style? Most academics, that's what they get off on, not ideas, they're only interested in...only the form. You're not so interested in form, you're interested in content—so am I. How much scope do you give to just the style per se? Not a lot?

CW: No, never in the sense that Anthony Burgess is obsessed by style. But...on the other hand you know I've always enjoyed the feeling of command over language. So...you know there are certain sentences in my books that I can go back over and it's a little 'ping'...

VR: Oh some brilliant imagery, brilliant imagery. You know especially some of the machine imagery. Tredell brings it out. You've sort of got this obsession almost, with man as machine. You have, you know, you talk about sort of vacuum pumps and things and different gears. Some of your imagery I would say, is actually quite brilliant. Some of the metaphors are very, very clever, but I'd also have to say the other side, that some of your style is very *laissez-faire*.

CW: Oh yes, sure.

VR: Couldn't give a toss.

CW: No. Absolutely, and what's more I have a feeling this is partly done deliberately. You get sentences in...where I've really let myself go like in *New Pathways in Psychology* which sort of leads up to that comment that there's something fishy about human existence. In other words I've got a strong feeling that writing should be a method of talking, should be colloquial.

VR: Yes and it is in your novels. I just wondered if you could sustain some of that brilliant imagery throughout a book it would be a real masterpiece, at least for the academics...what I'm saying because sometimes within a page you can write something very, very brilliant as I've said ten times, then something that's fairly mundane all in the same page...that's shattering and awesome. Why can't you keep that level up? I haven't really got any more questions. I've taken up enough of your time.

CW: That's all right.

VR: The only other question...I was going to ask about Marilyn Monroe. You've met Marilyn Monroe, what were your impressions of her? I ask this as a Kiwi male of 40!

CW: Well as I said in that piece I wrote about mescaline that she kept coming back to me very hard. It was obvious from the moment I met her that something clicked. When we were together in the Royal Court Theatre her husband and I were on stage...

VR: You left together at the end and she grabbed your hand...

CW: And she grabbed my hand. It was very obvious that she was very attracted to me and I was very attracted to her. It was just one of these things I always had it about little blondes...Ping!

VR: So had I. I was married to one.

CW: Yeah. You know 'ping' and this sort of feeling she really did...create this instantly in me, and there was something that happened instantly.

VR: What was she like as a person though?

CW: I didn't get the impression that she was terribly bright.

VR: A so-called dumb blonde?

CW: Yes, something of a dumb blonde and that's what I would have expected. I mean I've known one or two like this—who've been sort of delicious in bed and so on...But in a way would probably be a bit of a disappointment in a longer relationship. I mean I was fortunate when I was 22 I met Joy. I've been with Joy ever since. 40 years now.

VR: It's a long time.

CW: Yeah.

VR: I've got nothing else to say.

CW: You know basically I sometimes think one of the problems with human beings is we exaggerate the importance of sex. The truth, as all saints know, sex is interesting but has to be kept in its proper place.

VR: You say that in your hierarchy of needs *a la* Maslow. Sex just...ain't at the top. You've said that many times. How do you feel about all these compendiums of your stuff coming out, over and over again, regurgitations of all of your books? You can buy them in supermarkets and places like that. Do you feel that sort of cheapens you somehow?

CW: Well no, the main thing is simply that I did it to make some money for my kids.

VR: Exactly. You don't feel that sort of...because in New Zealand when I said I was coming over to speak to you a lot of them said: 'He wrote *The Occult*, eh. What's he done since?' There's this sort of poor impression of you...I don't think that of you at all, I mean their impression is poor...they think that you're a hack writer who churns out compendiums of Murders of the Thirties sold at supermarkets and stuff like this. Does that worry you a bit? That's a financial thing?

CW: No, no. When you grind away as long as I did, you don't worry about your public image.

VR: No you don't. The financial rewards you deserve at this age surely, after all the years of penury.

CW: Well I'm still in penury believe me. (Laughs). No...I told you I once met with Compton McKenzie and said: 'You must be very rich', and he said 'if I stopped writing I'd be starving in three months time.'

VR: It's like that though isn't it.

CW: Mm, yeah.

VR: Maybe they'll make a better movie of the *Metamorphosis...* book.

CW: That would be good.

VR: That horrible *Lifeforce*—an atrocious movie.

CW: What a movie. One of the worst ever made—an awful film.

VR: It was. It was shocking.

CW: That one was the worst...

VR: You wrote *Flash Gordon*, someone told me you wrote the screenplay there.

CW: I did the final screenplay for it, yes.

VR: Do you get many other screenplays to do?

CW: No.

VR: *Jurassic Park* would be interesting.

CW: Mm. Yeah.

Colin Wilson As Hydra

[First published in *Philosophy Now*,
issue 85, July/August 2011]

On June 26, 2011, the writer Colin Wilson turned 80. I believe
he has been seriously underrated and undervalued in his
homeland, as a philosopher, as a novelist, as a critic, and as a
polymath explorer into the sometimes eldritch realms of
human potential. Part of the reason for this lack of academic
and popular recognition within Britain and the US – he is
certainly vitally popular elsewhere – is because Colin Wilson
is something of a Hydra.

In Greek mythology, the Hydra had seven or nine heads,
stemming from one massive body. If one were to slice off any
head it would grow back. Indeed in some versions, two heads
would return. A similarly resilient and prolific beast, Wilson
is seen on TV, in the press, in any number of second-hand
bookshops in any number of formats, and now on DVD with
his *Strange is Normal*. Some of his more recent heads can
look rather bizarre, and are said by some to be uttering
gobbledygook. Others say he spreads himself too thinly, and
is always saying the same thing anyway. He himself is
succinct on this point: "Isaiah Berlin once said that there are
two kinds of writers, hedgehogs and foxes. He said the fox
knows many things, the hedgehog knows just one thing. So
Shakespeare is a typical fox; Tolstoy and Dostoevsky are
typical hedgehogs. Now, I'm a typical hedgehog. I know just
one thing, and I repeat it over and over again. I try to approach

it from different angles to make it look different, but it's the same thing."

The Hydra Heads of Colin Wilson

Outsider. Wilson's first book, published in 1956, was the excellent *The Outsider*, and he has been out there ever since, in a huge tangential orbit of his own.

Novelist. He's written novels in several different genres – science fiction, fantasy, realist, crime fiction – always subsumed under his philosophy, and mostly patterned in the modernist tradition, albeit Wilson is sometimes postmodern in the delivery of his message: his fictive forays often owe more to Derrida than Dickens, although he would disavow this connection.

Literary theorist. Wilson is a consistent theorist regarding how novels and poems should be both written (see, for example, his fine *Craft of the Novel*) and critiqued, via his own Existential Literary Criticism. In this critical theory, literary craft takes a back seat to approaching questions about the meaning of life, and how to live one's life more powerfully (which for Wilson means being more evolutionary in focus).

Paranormalist, albeit somewhat innocent and over-trusting, like Sir Arthur Conan Doyle. Both Conan Doyle and Wilson gave credence to the Cottingley fairies, for example. Wilson continues to seriously consider all sorts of what many would in a polite mood call "weird stuff, man."

Fantastic Anthropologist/Historian. There's a whole New Age Hydra head here. Space ships, Atlantis, a homosexual Shakespeare, mix themselves up in Wilson's more recent speculations out on the fringe. Although he has gained many fans there, he has also probably lost some of his earlier more philosophical adherents.

Colin Wilson as Hydra

Criminologist particularly fascinated with sex crime and heinous murders, which are the dark side of the evolutionary drive.

Over the years Colin Wilson has reared other heads too: *Sexologist, Musicologist, Playwright &Scriptwriter, Columnist & TV Personality, Family Man* and *Collector* of, among other things, books and music. Wilson however *never* sprouted the head of an Angry Young Man (he was not such an animal, despite being occasionally grouped with Kingsley Amis and John Osborne); university-trained academic (probably a good thing!); deliberate postmodernist (what a contradiction in terms); Feminist; Marxist; or post-colonially-aware Englishman.

I wish to concentrate on the two heads which are arguably his most significant: *Existentialist Philosopher* and *Romantic Mystic*.

Colin Wilson, Existentialist Romantic

Wilson's core ideas are explained in several books which he calls his 'Outsider Cycle', and which appeared in the 1950s and 60s. His is an English existentialism, remote from to the narrowly academic British linguistic empiricism of the 1960s. He is a unique phenomenon. For example, in Robert Solomon's book, *Existentialism* (2005), Wilson is the only British, let alone English, philosopher included, if we discount Harold Pinter as a philosopher. A French critic was quoted on the inside dust jacket of the original 1966 edition of Wilson's *Introduction to the New Existentialism* as calling it: "the first important contribution to Existentialism ever made by an Englishman." (As an ironic aside, there's now a Facebook page entitled 'Colin Wilson is a better philosopher than Sartre'!) Reviewing it in *The Irish Times*, Grattan Freyer wrote: "Anyone seriously concerned with twentieth-century values must make themselves familiar with Colin Wilson."

What then is Wilson saying? Generally, he wants an intensive and exhaustive survey of man's inner states. More specifically, Wilson's avowed aim in the *Introduction*, as in several of his earlier philosophical works, is to improve not only on what he calls 'Existentialism Mark One' (Kierkegaard, Heidegger, Sartre, Jaspers, Camus, etc), but on its immediate progenitor, the Romantic movement. "Existentialism *is* Romanticism, and Romanticism is the feeling that man is not the mere creature he has always taken himself for," he says.

Romanticism was an artistic, literary, and intellectual movement which began in the late 18th century as a reaction to Enlightenment rationalism and the growing hegemony of science. Lasting until the mid 19th century, it was a movement of men and women who sensed that there was 'more' to life – as experienced through the magnificence of Nature. It included poets such as Coleridge, Byron and Shelley, visual artists such as Blake and Turner, and writers as diverse as Goethe and H.D. Thoreau. It was marked by intense passion and the elevation of aesthetic feeling. Existentialism, which was born in the 19th century but became very prominent in the mid-20th with Jean-Paul Sartre, Albert Camus and Simone de Beauvoir, saw men and women as alienated, lonely creatures born into a universe which is coldly indifferent to us, rendering our values absurd and condemning us to an inescapable freedom and responsibility.

The difference between Wilson's New Existentialism and the intense emotional spasms of the Romantics (which never lasted for any length of time and thus led to despair, depression and early demise) or the insufferable negativity of

Colin Wilson as Hydra

Existentialism Mark One, is that the New Existentialism is based on optimism and positivity.

Wilson wants to build on the momentary earth-shattering epiphanies of the Romantics and renounce the unhappy stoicism of the earlier Existentialists to point the way to a permanently-expanded state of consciousness. Then humans – or at least some of them – will evolve exponentially into grandiose creatures of the mind, tapping our giant vista of internal freedom and what Wilson calls the objective values of existence – "there is a standard of values external to [everyday] human consciousness," he claims in the *Introduction*. As he points out, "everyday consciousness is a liar."

Here I want to cast in bronze what to me is Wilson's most significant Hydra head – the headmaster of the heads, if you will, the driving force of the Colin Wilson creature: Wilson is by nature both a Romantic and a Mystic. Elsewhere, particularly in my PhD, *Existential Literary Criticism and the Novels of Colin Wilson* (1996), I have categorized Wilson as a *bona fide* Romantic in disposition, outlook and corpus – something I believe he would not deny. I believe he is also an English Mystic in the line of William Blake, Thomas Traherne and George Fox (see my *Wilson as Mystic*, 2001, for example). A mystic is somebody who claims an awareness of some transcendent reality beyond the restrictions of everyday life, and who believes that this numinous realm can be explored only through some means other than scientific rationality – for example by introspection. New Existentialism is Wilson's attempt to delineate an Existentialism which expands into free-range mysticism. Indeed his mystical impetus all-too-often overwhelms clarity of logic, expression, and sense: he is impelled to paint what he senses, in wide and colourful stokes, and damn the details. This is a significant point about his work: Wilson writes intensely, compelled to convey his vision over and over again, to the extent that often clarity of terminology or rigid logical progression are not priorities.

Colin Wilson's Mystical Peaks

The American psychologist Abraham Maslow (1908-1970) developed a theory that people have what he called 'peak experiences'. These are moments of intense inspiration, love, happiness, insight or heightened consciousness, when the individual is in complete harmony with himself and his surroundings. Maslow said that people who have developed to their full potential have peak experiences often – perhaps even many times a day – while others have them less frequently. Wilson seized on this idea, seeing how well it fitted with his project to develop an emotionally positive existentialism. He asked: why not have peak experiences all the time, inculcated deliberately? Part of Wilson's mission is to promote the deliberate pursuit of peak experiences through focused thought.

Another key concept in this New Existentialist mission, *intentionality* derives originally from Edmund Husserl and phenomenology, and has become a central concept in philosophy of mind. Intentionality is the power of mental activity to be about or to stand for things or states of affairs. It refers to the directedness or deliberate attentiveness of consciousness. Wilson believes that all consciousness is intentional, even sub-consciousness, as "Intentionality...can exist on many levels."

Wilson then synthesizes Maslow and Husserl as the two poles of New Existentialism: the intentional examination of *consciousness itself* leads inevitably to extended peak experiences, and beyond. Here Wilson shows himself to be a Grand Illuminator of the works of others, welding together what seems discordant data. Two statements, from 1966 and 1988, together give a clear picture of his approach: "The New Existentialism consists of a phenomenological examination of consciousness" (*Introduction*). "If consciousness is intentional, then we can deliberately make it *more* intentional, and that the result would be a step in the direction of the mystic's insight" (*Essay on the New Existentialism*).

Wilson argues that the intentional nature of human thought proves that there's a transcendental ego, a self who aims the arrow of perception, emotion and intellect at something – a coherent, sometimes unconscious director behind the camera. To Wilson "the completely passive observer is a fallacy." This is where he thinks Sartre went wrong philosophically.

Wilson wants to philosophically reinstate the individual self; yet he also wants this self to be the avenue to the obliteration or overcoming of itself. This is rather a logical *faux pas*, I think, and I have written elsewhere (e.g. in *Postmodern Mysticism*, 2008) of the irony of Wilson's many descriptions – especially in his fiction – of the transcendental ego being completely expunged during mystical visions.

Positive and Negative Evaluations

Wilson is an outsider. The synthesis that is New Existentialism is not meant for most people, it seems: "no solution… can be immediately applied to the 'man in the street'. But then, this is hardly important," he says in the *Introduction*. He would argue that most people are nowhere near ready to be propelled into the next evolutionary ambit which he has discovered. There is a good deal of mind-mapping to do initially – tunnels must be dug into humanity's mental caverns, and rooms constructed with permanent frameworks, before any opening of the entry gates for all. Until we solidify or map out our phenomenologically-derived consciousness, man is not yet ready for visions such as Wilson's: for evolutionary reasons, we have built internal firewalls. But Wilson also takes it that much more recently man has also awakened to his inner freedom, and *contra* Heidegger's 'forgetfulness of existence', having become bored with being bored, has suddenly remembered his Being. Yet the final evaluation of the New Existentialism – and indeed, of Wilson's entire career – turns on whether he ever successfully maps out our inner selves. Does he give us the roadmaps to his sort of internal assessment of ourselves, and to the concomitant experiential fireworks of extended euphoric, free vision?

According to the extremely high standards which Wilson himself sets for Existential Literary Criticism, the answer has to be 'No'. He hints, rather than explicitly draws out for us, how we are to live at a self-aware peak. Yet he remains well worth taking seriously as a philosopher precisely because he concentrates on questions of supreme importance: What is life's meaning? Why are we here? What should we be doing about it? Thus I will concur with and only slightly paraphrase Matthew Coniam's piece back in *Philosophy Now* Issue 32, regarding not only the New Existentialism, but Colin Wilson's life's work: "He has managed to winch the worldview of humanist Existentialism free of the *impasse* of despair... this unique and iconoclastic English Existentialist is well worth the sometimes considerable effort."

Colin Wilson as Hydra

Finally, let me add a personal note. To me, Colin Wilson has endured as a philosopher who must always be remembered, if not for his solutions, then at least for his syntheses, and for his always asking the questions we must all face. The fact that he has done so in a generally otiose academic and critical environment in his own homeland only shows his tenacity. He explores a difficult territory that few even attempt and despite his 'failure' according to his own literary critical criteria, Wilson should be judged with words culled from his 1960 review of Albert Camus' *The Possessed*: "whatever ultimate criticisms can be levelled at his work, *he was better than ninety-nine percent of his contemporaries.*" Though I have several reservations against a wholehearted acceptance of his New Existentialism, and some concerns about the relevance of some of his later writings, this is my own estimation of Wilson. So three cheers for Colin Wilson! Happy birthday to him, too.

2011

Colin Wilson Obituary (1931-2013)

[First published in *Philosophy Now*,
Issue 101, March/April 2014]

The passing of Colin Henry Wilson (June 26, 1931 – December 5, 2013) leaves a large rent in the fabric of authentic (meaning fully committed and lifelong intransigent) existentialist philosophy, a pretty spartan tartan at the best of times. As *The Guardian* obituary of 9th December 2013 lamented: "He was Britain's first, and so far last, homegrown existentialist star." Wilson was also a compelling harbinger of multifarious previously unheard-of authors, and an ever enthusiastic and immensely readable proselytizer of myriad divergent leftfield ideas. He was however first and foremost a philosopher, and he maintained that "I consider my life work that of a philosopher, and my purpose to create a new and optimistic existentialism."

The existentialist work *The Outsider* (1956) was his first and indeed his most famous book, and even if Wilson didn't give full details as to how the positive existential state-of-mind he promoted was to be achieved, his 'New Existentialism' remains a lodestone in an increasingly bleak world peopled by the Dauphins of fundamentalist religions and the fundamentally anti-fundamentalist acolytes of Dawkins. Wilson's undoubtedly romantic impellent was to translate and codify his prime philosophic truth: that a person is greater than they think they are, and that, damn it, they should be doing something about evolving a lot faster – transmogrifying into the mighty being that they inherently are.

Colin Wilson Obituary

In this doctrine he travelled far beyond the existentialist negativities of Sartre and Camus, as well as far beyond the trivialities of much academic philosophy. As such, Wilson also remained a lifelong counter to (post-)structuralist and postmodernist writers such as Derrida: for Colin Wilson, mankind is not a passive pebble rattling around inside imposed discourses; he is rather the master of his truly intentional conscious self. Wilson's obsessive drive to relate everything to and from this profound inner nuclear warhead, his mystic overview of how things 'really should be', compelled him to write, transcribe, read, rave and produce prodigiously across two distinct centuries. Indeed he "exhilarated a generation with the bold possibilities of life" (Ken MacLeod, *Aeon Magazine*, 23 December, 2013).

Colin Wilson would accept the vast neutral materiality of the universe, but he would continue to maintain that man is pre-eminent: that it is the human transcendental ego which is the crux of existence, and not the external world. As he wrote: "And why are we here? In our moments of optimism and enthusiasm this is something we know instinctively. The purpose is to colonise this difficult and inhospitable realm of matter and to imbue it with the force of life… this world of matter is not our home. That lies behind us in another world. But for those with enough strength and imagination it will become our home. And when that happens the purpose of human existence will have been achieved" (*Dreaming to Some Purpose*, 2005). Similarly, in a 2003 online interview with Geoff Ward, Wilson proclaimed, "Our purpose in the world is eventually to enable spirit to conquer matter, to get into matter to such an extent that there is no longer any matter." It is a vision of Man as Evolutionary Hero.

Colin Wilson Obituary

Forever the Outsider figure, transcending both the Anglo-American and Continental philosophical poles and immersed deeply among the tendrils of his own lavish ontological jungle, it is this – his preaching and teaching of our evolution into something natural yet supernatural – for which we will remember him. So as time fumbles forward, I believe this *sui generis* philosopher will continue to garner ever more glowing revisions from excavations of *all* his massive creative goldmine from libraries, second-hand bookstores, the web, and his wide-ranging presence also on videotape, audiotape and DVD. Why? Because Wilson is unique in his consistent and determinedly never-ceasing promotion of the realisation of human potential and growth via the self-augmentation of consciousness. He never wavered in this mission, ever.

It is apposite to say something about how Wilson viewed death, because he came to strongly affirm that bodily demise is not the end, but rather a passing to elsewhere. He writes: "It is not my purpose to try and convince anyone of the reality of life after death: only to draw attention to the impressive inner consistency of the evidence, and to point out that, in the light of that evidence, no one need feel ashamed of accepting the notion that human personality survives beyond bodily death" (*Afterlife*, 2000). Wilson also quoted Peter Fenwick on the belief that "Mind may exist outside the brain and may be better understood as a field, rather than just the actions of neurons in the brain" (Ward interview). This refers to the survival of a purely transcendent mind or intellect beyond any corporeal status. In this Wilson wants to transcend existentialist Martin Heidegger's rather stoical appraisal of life as a flight towards death, stressing rather the drive toward far more life, the need for people to plunge more fully into the life-stream, as for example in his newly discovered and recently published essay from the 1970s, *Evolutionary Humanism and the New Psychology* (2013): "The threat of death – or any great emergency – has the power of unlocking the habit pattern of concentration upon objectives, and producing [an] overwhelming sense of 'gratitude for existence'." Here Wilson clearly points out how 'traditional' existentialism failed: it assumed suicide was somehow a freedom from responsibility, whereas in reality, suicide is merely bringing forward bodily death. Yet to Colin Wilson, by living one's life to the fullest positive potential – by maturing one's consciousness to the max – one may ultimately survive bodily demise as a fully-evolved conscious mind: "But I do feel, nevertheless, that life after death is basically true, that we don't actually die... it seems to me it's just a basic fact" (Ward interview).

2014

❀

Colin Wilson (1931-2013)

❀

[First published in *Philosophy Now*,
Issue 112, February/March 2016]

Colin Wilson was perhaps England's only famous
existentialist philosopher. Indeed, Robert Solomon's book
Existentialism (2004) includes Wilson as the sole British
representative of existentialism. (Here I'll pass over the many
other designations of Wilson, such as mystic, occultist,
criminologist, and so on, for his lasting philosophical
achievements eclipse his other interests.) However Wilson
attended no university, and achieved no academic
qualifications, despite Iris Murdoch trying to convince him of
the benefits of a university education; as he wrote in his
memoir *The Angry Years* in 2006: "She and I took an
immediate liking to one another... and when she learned that
I had not been to a university, offered to get me a scholarship
at Oxford, a suggestion I gratefully declined." Indeed Wilson
only went to academic institutions as an intermittent writing
fellow or a guest lecturer. The author of *The Outsider*, then,
was himself outside the mainstream, not only of English
philosophy, but of English academia too.

Wilson left school at sixteen and drifted through various
jobs while pursuing his dream of becoming a writer. By the
age of twenty-three he was sleeping rough on London's
Hampstead Heath to save money and writing in the British
Library by day. He started work on a book appropriately
called *The Outsider*, examining the role of excluded lonely
individuals in creating literature and art. Published in 1956

Colin Wilson (1931-2013)

when he was only twenty-four, this book exploded onto the cultural scene bringing Wilson lasting fame and, indeed, far too much early publicity. His following book was damned by the critics and he had a couple of run-ins with the press. He and his new wife then retreated to a rural cottage in the far reaches of Cornwall on the south-west coast of England. There they lived for the rest of his life, while he wrote and wrote.

Wilson was a particularly prolific author: he wrote almost 200 books, although by his own admission he was somewhat of a 'hedgehog'. He used Isaiah Berlin's classic distinction between foxes and hedgehogs in an interview with Geoff Ward in 2001: "The fox knows many things; the hedgehog knows just one thing. So, Shakespeare is a typical fox; Tolstoy and Dostoevsky are typical hedgehogs. I am a typical hedgehog – I know just one thing, and I repeat it over and over again. I've tried to approach it from different angles to make it look different, but it is the same thing."

Wilson *vs* The French

Wilson's philosophical position is best delineated in his 'Outsider Cycle' of seven books written between 1956 and 1966, with *Introduction to the New Existentialism* (1966) being perhaps his most important work of philosophy. Otherwise, philosophically, the later compilation of several of his philosophical essays entitled *Beneath the Iceberg* (1998) is notable for its concentrated attacks on French philosophy.

Most significantly, in these books, Wilson stresses that he's a *positive* existentialist philosopher – this is not a contradiction in terms. As such was always *au contraire* the pessimistic Continental existentialists such as Jean-Paul Sartre and Albert Camus (as further shown in the title of his tome *Anti-Sartre* of 1981) and the later French postmodernists, such as Jacques Derrida, whom he often derided. As he revealed to Ward: "once I grasped what *Derrida* was saying I began to *hate* him." There is an irony here, in that many of Wilson's novels read somewhat 'post-modernistically' as he so earnestly strived to express his version of existentialism through his fiction.

Why such opprobrium against Twentieth Century French philosophy? Because Wilson strongly believed that Camus, Sartre, Derrida *et al* had misrepresented the inherent potential of humanity – which he thought could evolve to a better state of being – and had instead either focused on a stoic resignation to the fate of man (Wilson rarely concentrated on the potential of women), or had strenuously stressed a complete disavowal of human potential. In the particular case of Camus, whom Wilson met in 1957, there is an anecdote which displays just how big a chasm existed between them:

> "Wilson pointed out to Camus that there were a number of places in his [Camus'] works where characters were actually 'overwhelmed with meaning'. Wilson asked Camus why he didn't pursue that personally, and Camus pointed to a Parisian teddy boy slouching past the window, saying: 'What is good for him must be good for me also.' Wilson... got very excited, and irritable in a way, and said, 'That's nonsense. Are you telling me Einstein shouldn't have produced the Theory of Relativity because a Parisian teddy boy wouldn't understand it?'"

Colin Wilson (1931-2013)

Wilson's Existentialism

What made Wilson's brand of existentialism so unique was his idiosyncratic incorporation of key ideas from the German proto-existentialist Edmund Husserl (1859-1938), such as '*époche*' or 'reduction', and – most importantly – 'intentionality'. For Husserl, intentionality meant that all human consciousness is *directed towards* or *about* something. Wilson agreed that all perception is intentional, but also drew from Alfred North Whitehead's notion of 'meaning perception' ('prehension') to further assert that the individual gives meaning to the world through their intentionality.

For Wilson, the completely passive observer is a myth. He was therefore particularly opposed to what we might call the 'passive' analysis of contents of consciousness by previous philosophers, notably René Descartes and David Hume, as well as Immanuel Kant and George Berkeley and much philosophy since – including what he termed the 'Existentialism Mark One' of the French. He felt that their passive understanding of consciousness had thrown philosophy completely off track. Through it, Descartes had introduced ultimate doubt with his *cogito ergo sum*; Hume went further along this sceptical route with his doubting of cause and effect; whilst Roland Barthes and his peers went even further along this trail to cast strong doubts on the possibility of any unfettered human agency – that is, of human freedom.

However, Wilson's interpretation of intentionality held that man could delineate his own state of consciousness, and moreover, could and should evolve into a more meaningful state via a rigorous 'bracketing-out' investigation of it, since meaning came from man and was not somehow imposed upon him by external things. By 'bracketing-out' (Husserl's

Colin Wilson (1931-2013)

'reduction'), Wilson meant a systematic – he called it a 'scientific' – analysis of human mental states which 'reduced away' any erroneous preconceived ideas. If all perception is intentional, then for Wilson, the only way forward is inward.

Wilson also wanted to appropriate and build on the earth-shattering epiphanic experiences of the Romantics to abnegate the resignation of the Continental existentialists, who were mired unhappily in their stoic resignation to contingency – a passive kowtowing to human inadequacy – and to instead build once and for all an impenetrable edifice of permanently attainable expanded consciousness. This expanded consciousness is the 'real' or 'true' consciousness, for *everyday consciousness is a liar*. For this goal of consciousness expansion, Wilson also drew on Abraham Maslow's notion of *peak experiences*, insisting that by appropriately analyzing and signposting consciousness, man could evolve into a state of permanent peak experience. The optimism of a peak experience then breeds further optimism and expansion of consciousness... thus epiphanies could become the norm for those who searched within themselves and strove to achieve Wilson's specific form of disciplined self-knowledge. Friedrich Nietzsche, for Wilson, was therefore one of the few philosophers worth studying, because of Nietzsche's eternal positivity about the possibility of human overcoming 'in spite of everything'. Wilson was thus temperamentally also very much an outsider, sailing well beyond the squalls of resignation and despair that beset many of his existentialist peers.

A statement Wilson made in 1988 in his *Essay on the New Existentialism* draws together his borrowings from Maslow and Husserl, and sums up his abiding philosophy concisely. He wrote that if "consciousness is intentional, then we can deliberately make it more intentional... the result would be a step in the direction of the mystic's insight."

Wilson's Transcendental Ego

Wilson is never great at detailing precisely how we can achieve this evolved consciousness. He never specifies the steps by which his new existentialism would complete a 'bracketed' examination of conscious experience. Indeed, he occasionally waxes and wanes about the possibility that psychotropic drugs could in some way aid consciousness-widening, whilst at the same time stressing that most people are just not yet ready for the broadening of their minds. He can be rather too vague at times. It would seem he agrees with Jean Gebser, who says in *The Ever-Present Origin* (trans. 1985) that man himself actually makes the chemical and neurological components of consciousness – that is, brains – explode into life, and for this reason, concentration as well as the will to work on developing inner mental states is tremendously vital. In fact, Wilson proclaimed in *Wholeness or Transcendence?: Ancient Lessons for the Emerging Global Civilization* (1992) that Gebser "seems to me possibly the most important thinker of the twentieth century." For both men, consciousness would actually seem to activate the brain, rather than the other way around. Thus for Colin Wilson there is very definitely a Transcendental Ego, or Higher Self, even if he often depicts a rather mystical disintegration of this self. Man is not merely a set of chemical nuts and bolts, nerves and synapses. So Wilson obviously also firmly disagrees with such thinkers as Francis Crick, Richard Dawkins and Daniel Dennett.

Colin Wilson (1931-2013)

Wilson's Linguistic Philosophy

Wilson did have considerable empathy with Twentieth Century language theorists such as Ludwig Wittgenstein and J.L. Austin, but thought they went nowhere wide enough in their consideration of language. The evolutionary way forward lay for Wilson not only in the expansion of consciousness, but just as importantly, in the concomitant expansion of language to describe this process. He said we will need to construct a whole new way of speaking to describe the yet-to-be codified subcranial discoveries. Interestingly enough, then, Colin Wilson was not only a unique positive existentialist, but also a sympathizer with British linguistic philosophy. Indeed he proselytized for a combination of language theory and new existentialism in one overall package, and firmly believed that he would be able to unite these two major streams of Twentieth Century philosophy. Wilson had set himself a very ambitious and original lifelong project, then: one that he always felt he continued to progress in, even as he later widened his intellectual range to look into other zones, such as in an ongoing investigation of the occult. (As a bit of an aside concerning language and consciousness, Derrida somewhat deconstructed Husserl. Husserl wanted to say both that intentionality precedes language, but also that intentionality is expressed via language. The difficulty is then that intentionality cannot be free of language, and is accordingly obscured or corrupted – this is Derrida's *différence*. Wilson attempts to explain this away in a piece entitled 'Notes on Derrida for Rowan' in *Below the Iceberg*. There, regarding Derrida, he states, "if he is arguing that the inbuilt ambiguity of language can never be pinned down, then he is merely siding with various other sceptics and relativists, and needs to be taken no more seriously than they are… There are only two pockets on the billiard table of philosophy, and Derrida has undoubtedly landed us back in the one labelled 'David Hume'.")

Wilson Ultimately

Colin Wilson remains truly one of a kind, and well worthy of study both within and without the institutions that have largely disavowed or even forgotten him. The New Existentialism – Wilson's way to achieve the ultimate quasi-mystical apotheosis of consciousness – necessitates an approach whose methods might even ultimately be described as Anglo-Saxon and empirical rather than as Continental and purely rationalist.

A journalist once asked Wilson if he thought he has had any influence as a philosopher, to which he replied "none at all." However his 'phenomenological metaphysics' – as it was described by the critic Cacturimus in an issue of *The Minnesota Review* of 1967 – bears serious re-evaluation.

2016

Colin Wilson: more than the existentialist outsider

Introduction:

I wish to concretize once and for all, Colin Wilson's rightful place as a philosopher. More than this, as an important philosopher, who not only introduced his own version of Existentialism, but also strove to unite the so-called Continental and Analytic traditions of philosophy into one seamless endeavour, via his stressing that descriptive language is as much a bedrock of a phenomenological approach as are reductions and a focus on essences. His prima facie importance as an original philosopher, can not and should not be underestimated.

I will commence this piece evaluating the philosophic lifework of Wilson, with four incremental statements of his import, given that everything else he wrote stemmed from his basic philosophical impetus anyway.

One: Wilson is a *bona fide* philosopher *per se*. This was accepted, if not at the time of his earlier writing when he penned the seven volume Outsider Cycle, but most certainly later. Thus, for example, Shand, Moorhouse and Dossor wrote early separate Paupers' Press booklets identifying him as such; while he is also listed in *The Continuum Encyclopaedia of British Philosophy* (2006).

While Shand (2004) also mentions admirers of Wilson— among them being Roger Scruton, Steve Taylor and Stephen Clark—noting that, "he is not without admirers within the philosophy profession."

More than the Existentialist Outsider

More, even the usually disparaging Collini (2006) rather begrudgingly admits, "To decide who should be described as 'the best-known philosopher in Britain in the 1950s', one would have to spend some time on the preliminaries of definition and boundary-setting....there can be no doubt that if the criterion of being 'well-known' is commercial success, then the answer has to be, improbably, Colin Wilson."

Then there is Ree's earlier similarly off-hand ranking of him in 1993, "Russell, Ayer and Joad were by far the best-known philosophers of the 50s—apart from Colin Wilson, that is."

Significantly also, Wilson himself was very interested, more especially in his younger years, in mainstream British philosophy, as is evidenced in his writing incisive and generous commentaries about several English 'mainstream' philosophy luminaries such as Broad, Ayer, Strawson, Warnock and Popper in a *Daily Telegraph* feature in 1968. He also wrote as a cover blurb for Brian Magee's *Modern British Philosophy* (1971), "The whole book has a marvelous air of casualness and clarity that makes it a delight to read."

His further, less salubrious commentaries on continental thinkers such as Foucault, Derrida and, earlier, their countrymen such as Sartre and Camus, also occupied prominent space in his oeuvre over quite some time up into the 21st century, as best summarized in books such as *Below the Iceberg* (1998). Take, for example, his comment to Theroux in 2002 about Derrida, where he stated that he spent two years getting to grips with Derrida, "I was determined to crack this fucker," before he went on to deprecate Foucault in even more earthy terms. While there is certainly some truth in James Marshall's 2004 and 2006 criticisms of the polemical, "broad-brush confrontationist" way Wilson depicted the work of Camus, for example, and other French thinkers, this was because Wilson was still very intent on countering what he saw as these thinker's abiding negative philosophies.

Colin Wilson, then, certainly viewed himself as a philosopher. One only has to flick through the recent compendium of his writings about an assortment of thinkers, as edited by Colin Stanley, *Collected Essays on Philosophers* (2016) to see his abiding interest and commitment. His own self-summation in the essay also entitled 'Below the Iceberg', reinforces this, "Up until the late 1960s, I had considered myself a kind of 'existentialist' philosopher, who was attempting to rescue existentialism from the pessimism of Sartre, Camus, and Heidegger," before his self-confessed swing toward the occult.

Given that Shand (2016) notes that, "Colin Wilson has found virtually no place in university academic philosophy"; as a measure of how Wilson is now acccptcd by the British philosophical community, one only has to look at the Philosophy Now journal, where Wilson has—increasingly, I might add—been written about positively; including by myself, across several issues. In short, nowadays he is indeed seen by an increasing number of his peers as a philosopher above all else and as worthy of mention as other British philosophers—who remain even now primarily entrenched in their so-called analytic tradition, one still including Logical Positivists and Language Philosophers.

Two: Wilson was an English Existentialist philosopher, indeed probably the only one, although we could perhaps also add the names of Alfred North Whitehead (at Wilson's own behest), Iris Murdoch, R.D. Laing and Herbert Read to this tiny list. Wilson appears in the 2012 *Cambridge Companion to Existentialism*, while much earlier, Ree described him in these words, "Colin Wilson was a native outsider, a homegrown existentialist...England's own existentialist" (1993). Solomon's anthology *Existentialism* (2004) also includes Wilson as essentially England's sole representative; if we disregard a dramatic interlude-excerpt from Harold Pinter. Appignanesi (2002) and Coniam (2001) confirm this opinion, as the latter articulates so well, "that rarest of creatures, an English Existentialist." Woessner (2012) further adds to the mix, by stating, "In Wilson, Britain at last had its very own, native-born Sartre...Wilson was even better than Sartre for the popular press because he was no Parisian cafe-sitting intellectual," a summative sentiment further reinforced by *The Guardian* newspaper 2013 obituary with the definitive statement, "Britain's first homegrown existentialist star".

While in Europe itself, writers such as an anonymous French critic was quoted on the inside dust jacket of the original 1966 edition of Wilson's *Introduction to the New Existentialism* as calling it, "the first important contribution to Existentialism ever made by an Englishman." A Romanian, Stefan Ion Bolea more recently wrote, "...the Anglo-Saxon space did not produce a single existentialist philosopher (with the possible exception of Colin Wilson)".

Finally, Sarah Bakewell's somewhat dismissive and rather discursive summary of Wilson in *At the Existentialist Café* (2016) does at least include him in the ranks of serious Existentialist thinkers. An attribution, Wilson would certainly have concurred with. While Bakewell seems not to have even opened *Introduction to the New Existentialism*, Wilson's key text from 1966, she does at least write, "The English 'new existentialist' Colin Wilson lived until 5 December, 2013...retaining the loyalty of many international readers who had been excited and enlightened by his books. One can leave worse legacies in the world."

Again, there is mutual agreement as to Wilson's place as an English Existentialist, perhaps the sole such, and certainly the only one who wrote their own philosophy books expressing this philosophy.

Three: Wilson was a unique Existentialist philosopher for two key reasons. One: because of his perpetual positiveness, which straight away set him apart from other European existentialists. Two—and perhaps most tellingly—his willingness to accommodate the Language Philosopher's call for a rigorous analysis of language. His forthright statement in *Beyond the Outsider* (1965) was, "The way forward lies through the development of language". It is this very significant aspect of his philosophy I will soon concentrate on, for this aspect has never been sufficiently scrutinized, if at all. Firstly, however, more as regards Wilson as an unique existentialist philosopher and his abiding positiveness. Wilson's (New) Existentialism is *sui generis* precisely because it is so optimistic, as reflected in Spurgeon's title, *Colin Wilson: Philosopher of Optimism* (2006) and as affirmed by authors like Bertonneau who wrote in 2011, "what he has created…is a positive existentialism—or what would be more accurately described nowadays as a kind of 'transpersonal existentialism'." Another who has latterly written on this aspect of Wilson's existentialism, is Montgomery (2016), with his commentary about Wilson, "He liked to think of himself as an optimistic existentialist...If he were here I think what he would say is, 'Who among you will write the next great existential novel or the next great existential book? If not one of you, then who?' That would be Colin Wilson's attitude towards our potential."

Now, this aspect of Wilson's existentialism has been well covered by other writers, as well as by myself, and includes delineation of Wilson's several stepping stones to a fully realized consciousness, namely an understanding of the transcendental ego, peak experiences, intentionality. A good summary of his affirmativeness is in Shand's 2005 review of Solomon's *Existentialism*, in which he devoted most of the review to Wilson, as following, "One in the collection who deserves far greater attention than he usually gets." He then goes on, "Wilson's challenge is: why should we be so prone to think that a view of the world that lacks value is the true one?...we don't have to be passive; we can do things to our consciousness awareness...Wilson's quest has been to learn how to sustain such yea-saying states."

Thus the hallmark of Wilson's New Existentialism, as best contained in a handful of titles bearing this term, was his manifest disdain for the negativity of continental existentialists such as Sartre and Camus and his demand for mankind to phenomenologically examine their own consciousness as the fundamental necessity prior to his/her finally attaining a vast and vatic vision. Evolution was his mantra; not the dystopic pessimism of his continental peers, let alone the closed minds of his fellow countrymen, whether they be philosophers or not. Wilson was entirely alone and apart. His embodied own best Outsider, in fact and practice.

Second and most significantly for this piece, Wilson also saw the requirement to incorporate a disciplined new language, to invent a new terminology and therefore to incorporate a concomitant linguistic analysis as vital to this New Existentialism. It is this component, which places Colin

More than the Existentialist Outsider

Wilson even further beyond his own apocalyptic existentialist outsiders, even the few such dynamic and ultimately yea-saying visionaries such as Nietzsche, Wilber et al.

Wilson was, then, literally outside the outsider; in fact, on a distinct tangent away even from other existentialists. As Neil Griffiths wrote in 2007, "He was always an outsider in the U.K." Now he can be viewed as doubly outside, as it were, by virtue of his abiding philosophy, which sought to take on board a staunch analysis of language as the precursory and complementary method of developing his unique and overridingly affirmative existentialist credo.

Wilson as a Language Philosopher? No, surely not! Well, actually, yes indeed.

Throughout his earlier, younger writing—well-before a swoop into the occult and other rather esoteric topoi—Wilson did quite consistently applaud analytical language phil-osophers—believe it or not. Thus, he is accommodating of Wittgenstein, whom he wrote about across several books such as *Religion and the Rebel* (1957), *Beyond the Outsider* (1966) and in his own autobiography, *Voyage to a Beginning* (1969), and even J. L. Austin and his *Sense and Sensibilia* in particular, as commented on in Wilson's own *New Pathways in Psychology* (1972).

Wilson writes, "The school of linguistic philosophy—whose key figures are Wittgenstein and J. L. Austin—has recognized the inadequacy of 'everyday' language…Austin's 'philosophy' represents an attempt to 'tighten up' language to an unprecedented degree, with minute concentration upon the function of words…This is obviously an important and necessary approach" (*Introduction to the New Existentialism*, 1966).

More than the Existentialist Outsider

"Wittgenstein was a great forerunner...he aimed at doing foundation work on which it would be possible to build a philosophy" (*INE*).

"In the *Philosophical Investigations*...Wittgenstein makes a good beginning...Words are of as many different types...we have no system of classifying them...Most of Wittgenstein's work after the *Tractacus Logico-Philosophicus* is concerned to make his readers aware of the nature of language. To destroy the 'natural standpoint' in which language is accepted as a 'comprehensive description of reality" (*Beyond the Outsider*, 1966).

"Austin...agreed with the later Wittgenstein that most philosophical problems have defied solution because our language is too slipshod" ('The Thinkers', 1968).

An irony here, however, is summed up by Ree (1993), in that J. L. Austin was no fan of Wittgenstein, "Austin did not take Wittgenstein very seriously." In fact, Austin rather disparagingly called Wittgenstein, 'Witters', while Wittgenstein was only ever recorded as attending one Austin seminar. Oddly, however, there are considerable similarities in their approach to language, given that one was a quintessential European and the other a quintessential Englishman!

Wilson certainly agreed with the language philosophers about the requirement for a structured linguistic approach, given that Wilson went well beyond and away from what he perceived as the ultimately limited parameters of analytic and positivist philosophy. As Rycroft (2010) wrote in his book *Swinging City*, "For...Wilson...then, logical positivism in its political and aesthetic form was the rationalist philosophy which was not only emblematic of technocracy, but tended to narrow down the areas about which it was safe to speculate".

For him, "Personally I am out of sympathy with the Oxford philosophers. What they are doing seems to me extremely interesting, but far too narrow, and the results it achieves are disappointingly small…There is certainly not a philosopher in England today who would agree with me" ('The Thinkers' 1968). I feel his summation about himself here, to be without doubt, as well as especially apt.

For him linguistic analysis was, however, an intrinsic and initial component of erecting a vast existential superstructure. Yes, he concurred with and even applauded thinkers such as Austin, who believed in the rigorous scrutiny of 'ordinary and reasonably practical' language and called for a detailed study of the language we use to speak about something and of the way that we use it. However, Wilson wanted to inaugurate a far wider spectrum of specific language—as a symbiotic component of the exploration and thus, the extension of human consciousness.

In other words, Wilson wanted to make such supposedly exceptional terminology into everyday language, just as an 'advanced' consciousness was, in fact, the true 'normal'.

Again, "The valuable part of logical positivism is its objection that imprecision of language has prevented philosophy from achieving its aim. When it declares that it is neither possible nor desirable to 'see things as a whole', it is merely invalidating itself with self-contradiction. The nature of philosophy is to grope towards this 'bird's-eye view," (*Voyage to a Beginning*).

Wilson and the need for [a new] language.
So, although Wilson shared with Logical Positivists *et al* the need for intensive language analysis, this was all imperative for his far more wide-ranging positive vision, given that it was

fundamental to it. Yet, the Language School et al did not share a wide-range vista at all, because for him, although "Existentialism is always preoccupied with a sense of the inadequacy of language...language must be developed until it is no longer inadequate," (*INE*) he insisted man must and can and does travel further. It is important to note that Wilson did not see this internal mapping and naming as an easy task, indeed it is analogous, "to building a road into the wilderness" (*ibid*).

"The point of phenomenological existentialism is not the peak experience; it is the control of consciousness and its extension by language...At the moment, language is an unconscious slave of consciousness. It assumes it possesses a precision that it does not, in fact, possess, for it has tried to build its precision upon this quicksand of variable consciousness. If it is to serve its function, it must take into account the mechanisms of varying consciousness. Consciousness must be mapped and defined," (*Voyage to a Beginning*).

Again, "nevertheless the point should be made here that a phenomenology of language is as vital to the development of a new existentialism as the phenomenology of values," (*INE*). This is perhaps his key quotation to note.

Wilson then, uniquely tried to amalgamate the then prevailing analytic language-based philosophy, most especially this aspect of logical positivism that was at its genesis, into his own firebrand existentialist pantheon. He actually wanted to unite two apparently divergent philosophical poles, as per this further important quote from his 1966 masterwork, "Not the least important feature of the 'new existentialism' is that it is able to unite the two major traditions of twentieth century philosophy: linguistic empiricism and phenomenological existentialism".

No one else approached this goal, let alone came near to even enunciating it. Indeed, few other thinkers have even remarked on this combination of existentialism and language philosophy. More, I have found the only external reference of succinct note is the following: "As superficial as his discussion is, Colin Wilson was one of the first English writers to have devoted much attention to a comparison between the two schools…and his *Introduction to the New Existentialism* (1966) remains virtually the only attempt to synthesise various aspects of the two schools into a new philosophical approach," Maurice Roche (2013).

I will, return to this significant summation further on.

So, what was this new language 'all about', then?
As earlier touched on, Wilson's new/positive existentialism demanded a systematic phenomenological examination of mental states or stages of consciousness, most especially what he termed 'abnormal inner states', because these are the lodestar toward a more developed consciousness, from which will ultimately evolve a completely awakened being consistently experiencing what he termed peak experiences (from Maslow). Such widening of consciousness would be instigated by harnessing one's intentionality. This is a term from Husserl; although Wilson gives this concept his own special spin and nominates the term as an individuals' meaning-giving implant into any activity, perceived or conceived.

This mapping of such advanced stages and states of consciousness, themselves variable—this 'science of consciousness'—itself rigorous and painstaking, will necessitate at the same time, a whole new language so as to describe and delineate and pin down what is going on and at the same time would actually enhance these states. Mankind simply does not yet have the words to describe specifically these advanced aspects of consciousness, such as mysticism and even drug-induced hallucinogenic ones. Thus, "the 'new' language of existentialism will be created out of a patient attempt at phenomenological description of man's inner states" - particularly the abnormal inner states -"a 'new existentialism' must begin with the rather pedestrian task of pushing its scaffolding of language into these new realms"(*INE*).

The implicit irony then, is that Wilson himself saw the demarcation of new terms in these words, "Its methods might be described as Anglo-Saxon and empirical rather than as 'continental' and 'metaphysical'" (*ibid*). The parallel to logical positivism is obvious, while his statement establishes him even further as revolutionary—for although the genesis of phenomenology was indeed from the European continent, his is an original and very English, positive analytical existentialism! This is no non sequitur either—it is where he was traveling, intent and focused on his own route. The fact that for Wilson, his working within the English language and his non-reference to any other languages, further solidifies this Anglophile vision, if you will.

More clarificatory quotations:
"My disagreement with Freudian psychology and logical positivism is not directed against their positive aspects (i.e. their heuristic aspects): it is more often an irritation with the positivist who declares confidently that it is all right with him if the map never gets filled in" (*The Strength to Dream*, 1962). Again, Wilson shared with analytical language philosophers

the initial requirement to pin down words, but stressed the need to go much further, to invent new ones that had cogency as consciousness became increasingly investigated. He demanded that mankind press ever on to unravel metaphysical reality, once and for all—a task he would have posited that language philosophers deemed as meaningless and beyond their gambit. (Interestingly enough however, an anonymous *Times Literary Supplement* (1967) reviewer of Wilson's own *Introduction to the New Existentialism* did point out that, "the view that most philosophers of the school of linguistic analysis 'regard religious questions as meaningless' is merely grotesque.")

"It must be emphasized that the investigation of these [semi-mystical] states is largely a problem of language...It is all a question of using phenomenology—'the descriptive analysis of subjective states'—to create a real psychology, and creating a language capable of pinning down these elusive mechanisms of consciousness, " (*Voyage to a Beginning*).

"To speak of phenomenology is to speak of the limitations of language in describing man's inner processes...A positive existentialism should begin from an awareness of the limitations of language...Our language at present is little better than a primitive sign language" (*Beyond the Outsider*). Again, Wilson here draws on Wittgenstein as at least considering how best to develop language.

Similarly, for Wilson, language is, "adulterated with preconceptions and fallacies,"(*ibid*) and we must work hard developing a new, meaningful one. "All this is foundation work. The real work still lies ahead," (*ibid*). What was required was akin to a linguistic drill that could not bend as it bored into the nether realms of consciousness. Again, "language is the drill…The way forward lies through the development of language" (*ibid*).

Does Wilson actually commence the work?

Colin Wilson was very good at generalizations and rather sweeping conclusions. The question must now be asked: given that his prognosis about the requirement for a measured, structured and vital exploration of consciousness and at the same time developing new technical vocabulary to define these states, did he actually give us some clues as to how to even commence this exquisitely complex task? He certainly attempted to concretize steps towards this goal, as in his 6-part set of recordings entitled *The New Analytic Philosophy* from 1967—here to "develop phenomenological insights into a practical Western discipline toward the pursuit of higher consciousness." Note the title and the intrinsically analytic aspect.

Indeed, when one listens to these tapes, as I have done at the Colin Wilson Archive at the University of Nottingham, one is riveted by Wilson's important statements from side A of tape four. As here: "It's language that's at fault." He goes on to talk about how language always develops in a way similar to the way a building goes up—to start with a conceptual framework, then to place bricks (words and concepts) inside this framework. However, Wilson laments that, "our current conceptology is 200 years out of date." We need to introduce new concepts, to completely clear out old foundations and to lay new such, which he claims he has been doing, "in all my books." He speaks enthusiastically about the enormous housekeeping to be done regarding ideas and language, akin to, "trying to clean up a room that has been allowed to get dirty for two centuries." What is required are big, new concepts, new words, which Wilson admits to inventing in his attempt to reclassify expanded states of consciousness.

Other than this reconstruction with a completely new set of (verbal) materials, how else does he direct us? Overall, the best approach he suggests is something like the 'frame method', as in *Beyond the Outsider*. This would consist of an incredibly patient, consistent and methodical exploration of consciousness in all its manifold forms, including mystical states, and the tracking of each and every iota of data—and at the same time giving each one a name—thus building up a meaning network. Wilson here admits here that, "Language has not, so far, succeeded in labeling this complex 'flow and recoil' of our responses to experiences, to the ultimate unraveling of the problem of human existence," (*ibid*).

John Shand (1996) concurred entirely, "A reason, according to Wilson, why these 'peak experiences' have not been imported into our lives to give it meaning and purpose is that we do not have the language to articulate their nature…It should be the aim of our intellectual evolution to construct such a language." Shand also inculcates Wittgenstein's Private Language Argument here, whereby, "certain artistic and scientific acts of creativity cannot occur until the language in which they can be articulated has been developed", while Lachman (2016) adds, "Wilson believes in language's ability to capture and analyze reality…he aims at greater precision".

Further implications.

It is essential to note that Wilson also wrote a plethora of fiction, as a key way of also being a philosopher. For him, a basic reason for writing novels was that, "They are also a manner of philosophising...I am almost tempted to generalise and say that no philosopher is qualified to do his job unless he is also a novelist...I would certainly exchange any of the works of Whitehead or Wittgenstein for the novels they ought to have written," (*Voyage to a Beginning*).

Through his fiction, Wilson strove to delineate his phenomenological existentialism via his many descriptive passages of 'advanced' states of consciousness, which—while imaginatively capturing such experiences—did not essentially inculcate the specific steps whereby the experience was achieved, and delineated rather these 'semi-mystical' states as complete in themselves. (See Rapatahana, 1995 and 2001, for further examination of what I would describe as Wilson's mystical adumbrations).

As a closely related point regarding his fictive work, I mentioned earlier Wilson's own efforts to invent and inaugurate new words and phrases that—for him—described such states of consciousness, as experienced by him during his own life. For example, 'St Neot Margin'. 'Ladder of Selves'. 'Dual Value Response'. 'Faculty X'. 'The Laurel and Hardy Theory of Consciousness'. 'The Indifference Threshold.' These are but a trickle of his non-fictional terminologies, as he consistently strove to articulate such experiences in a meaningful way, to enhance further their essence via his own new terminology, and—importantly—to communicate the meaning of this phraseology to others. In his novels too several of his fictional characters undergo similar transcendental experiences, whereby Wilson attempted to convey men themselves transported beyond mundane reality and limited states of awareness. Here he created whole other scenarios and settings such as the black room, the personality surgeon, the space vampires, the mind parasites—as just some further attempts to advance his agenda.

More than the Existentialist Outsider

Wilson, then, was fascinated not only by states of consciousness in all their variegated forms, but also in quantifying novel words and phrases that could somehow capture them, pin them down to be dissected and then built from. His frustration as an affirmative philosopher, a man who himself entered and experienced quasi-mystical states, in not being able to completely linguistically depict what he had experienced, must—at times—have been palpable. Indeed he must have been continually torn between the analytical 'Anglo-Saxon; side of his brain and the instinctive mystical bent that propelled him ever on. Perhaps, then, his system of philosophy could be described in exactly the same way he described the work of Heidegger in *Beyond the Outsider*. Namely, as Howarth-Williams writes about the German, not via, "systematic, rigorous logically consistent propositions; but comprehensible, illuminating…emotive, 'pointing-towards' language, rather than analytic-descriptive, representational language."

There is some irony, then, in a point made by Schofield (2013), who stated, "Colin Wilson has written that we use words in an attempt to 'digest' our experiences, and that at times we suffer from indigestion. At such times analytical philosophy is taken as a kind of 'Alka-Seltzer.'"

In other words, while striving to pin down states of consciousness, the evolutionary platforms to ascend, one by one, Wilson was himself constrained by the semantic gap between concretizing what he felt, what he experienced in a new language; and the actual experience as pertaining. His actual words ex-Schofield above, are, "You might say that words are an attempt to 'digest' our experience; if they don't perform this function, because they are used in artificial or highfalutin' ways, the result will be severe indigestion. Most philosophy is simply an attempt to supply Alka Seltzer." (Introduction to 'The Thinkers'). The ineffability of extended states of consciousness all too often led to the realization that our language—as yet and even despite his own articulated inventions of terminology—was still imperfect in capturing them once and for all.

Indeed, it is this very gap between language and therefore knowledge, and any direct contact with 'reality', that lead to thinkers such as Derrida. Thinkers who continued to intensely probe this schism between reality and our experience of it; to nit-pick the inherent and inevitable ambiguities of language—so as to arrive at a state whereby nothing made sense other than this endemic no sense. In other words, Derrida diced up language, further than even Austin would allow for.

Austin posited, "that language has deeper dimensions besides a correspondence to the world, and that this 'locutionary' force is only a limited part of the spectrum of language," (Listik, 2015). This was the very thing that initially drew Derrida's attention to Austin, however Derrida went far further, radically so, when he stated that Austin was far too narrow in his purview of language by his excluding what the latter called 'parasitic speech acts.'

Derrida inevitably draws the ire of Colin Wilson. "Derrida's philosophy...has called attention to the inevitable gaps to be negotiated between experience and reality, especially in relation to our use of language, and however small-scale we make our scrutiny," (Benson, 2014).

Now Wilson, despite sighting these semantic gaps himself and his striving to abridge them via his own jargon, found Derrida *et al*, insufferable, for not seeing the wider wood of expanded human consciousness for all the word trees they had cut down. For trivializing into absurdity the role of language.

More than the Existentialist Outsider

As Wilson ('Notes on Derrida for Rowan', 1998) himself points out, "It seems to me that Derrida is overdoing the complications. All writers know about the ambiguity of language: Eliot says 'Words slide, slip, crack under the strain.' But "linguistic slippage" isn't really cause for a kind of defeatism."

And here, where Wilson deconstructs Derrida to a degree, "Language, according to Derrida, is a bit like the surface of the sea. No waves are permanent, they move continually...the 'inbuilt ambiguity of language'" (*ibid*). He then constructively responds to Derrida's gulf with, "Words are not really notes of music; they differ in one respect: that they do have 'dictionary meanings'...since a word does have that basic foundation of 'dictionary meaning', its 'ambiguity' isn't really all that serious...it could be made finally 'unambiguous'" (*ibid*).

Or as Bertonneau (2016) clarified, "Wilson observes that Derrida has constructed a bad syllogism: Just because ambiguity is one characteristic of language, it never follows that language is nothing but ambiguity, or, in Derrida's coinage, jeu or 'play.'"

Interestingly, Wilson parallels Wittgenstein in the latter's disavowal of Derrida. As Gier (2007) points out, "Wittgenstein's general project is to reconstruct language at work, but Derrida's strategy is to deconstruct the alleged workings of any language." For Wittgenstein, "there will be common ground, the bedrock of a shared world-picture that makes communication among...cultural worlds possible," (*ibid*)—which is exactly the position of Wilson as regards language.

Wilson's later scorn for Barthes, Foucault, Derrida and so on, at the same time emphasizes his continued and career-long interest in the importance of language *per se*—well after the 'Outsider Cycle'. Given this and given his call for a rigorous phenomenological examination of conscious-ness as tied directly to a relational vocabulary that is cogent and clear, it bears noting how he replied when Green (2004) interviewed him. Said Green, "I express surprise that he's not interested in experimenting with language and structure in the avant-garde mode, as ways of exploring altered states of consciousness." Wilson responded by pointing out that he was more interested in first getting across his basic ideas.

Indeed and essentially still, "The real work still lies ahead," (*Beyond the Outsider*).

Summary

To sum up: For Colin Wilson, we will need to construct a new way of speaking and writing, so as to fully describe the essence of the yet-to-be codified sub-cranial discoveries. Thus the requirement for new words, and new concepts that precisely capture suchlike. This vital imperative to have such linguistic expression, which expresses firmly and finally not just what we consciously experience but is communicable for everyone and not just the experiencing individual, is well defined in a quotation from Wilson's own *The Philosopher's Stone*. Here a dullard suffers a head wound, but cannot express the concomitant vision he then has, "We had found someone who could plunge into ecstasy as a moment's notice. Here was a Wordsworth without the power of self-expression, a Traherne who could only say 'Gor, ain't it pretty.'" In other words, any vivid states of consciousness experiences have also to be communicable to others, via a representative language.

More than the Existentialist Outsider

We at the same time must undertake a careful bracketing-out process whereby inner states of whatever ilk (including also madness and sexual ecstasy) are identified, isolated and made relational to other such states.

In this careful voyage within, Wilson promises that mankind will ultimately extend their consciousness so vastly that whole new meaning-horizons will become natural to us—or to those who make the twofold phenomenological/language analysis mission their purpose. In his own words, words, which sum up his entire pantheon, "The new existentialism consists of a phenomenological examination of consciousness" (*INE*). To which we may well add, 'And at the same time the construction of a dictionary of new and revelatory words and phrases.'

With such a lexical map in hand, this bright burning star then is his duo-credo: "If consciousness is intentional, then we can deliberately make it more intentional [1966], and that the result would be a step in the direction of the mystic's insight" [1988].

Wilson was, then, outside the outsider in so many inter-connected ways. Outside physically (for he lived most of his life well away from urbanization; close to the sea). Outside intellectually and temperamentally (as via his continuously repeated and passionately expressed positive ideas in his massive lifework, across all genre). And outside as a sui generis affirmative analytic English Existentialist (for no one else saw—or has seemed to see since—the requirement to conjoin a cohesive language philosophy with a philosophy of being, as necessary precursor to evolution.)

Colin Wilson, then, remains ever an unique Existentialist Outsider Philosopher.

More than the Existentialist Outsider

Coda

Yet, *inter alia* what I have written about above, there is an interesting bond-connection to another philosopher who shared some similar extended views as did Colin Wilson— and whose name Wilson even incorporated into two of his novels, as key characters pursuing evolutionary consciousness. (Thus Gilbert Austin in *The Mind Parasites*—where Gilbert must surely also refer to Ryle—and earlier in *Ritual in the Dark*—Austin Nunne!)

Linguistic Phenomenology is J. L. Austin's term as characterizing his own philosophical approach, which is generally called linguistic philosophy or ordinary language philosophy. Austin claimed that discussing the functions of certain words and sentences and inventing new ways of describing phenomena is not merely linguistic, but improves our perception of reality or phenomena on the basis of a sharpened awareness of words. Hence, it should be considered to be a sort of phenomenology. "When we examine what we should say when, what words we should use in what situations, we are looking again not merely at words (or 'meanings', whatever they may be) but also at the realities we use the words to talk about ... For this reason I think it might be better to use, for this way of doing philosophy...for instance, 'linguistic phenomenology', only that is rather a mouthful." (Austin, *Philosophical Papers*, 1961).

The similarities of Austin's articulation of a linguistic phenomenology to Wilson's new existentialism, as refined in his own words several times earlier and again as below, are manifest. Given that the language philosopher, Austin, begins with analyzing words and travels somewhat towards essence and the phenomenologist, while Wilson, calls for an analysis of words as an integral and synchronous component of a phenomenological existential voyage. As again here: "Genuine 'new language' is so difficult to create. It is analogous to building a road into the wilderness...Far from being 'unscientific,' Existentialism is a logical extension of the idea of a scientific philosophy...Existentialism is always preoccupied with a sense of the inadequacy of language...language must be developed until it is no longer inadequate" (Wilson, *INE*).

In the end, then, Colin Wilson and J. L. Austin had more than a fair bit in common. For example, consider what Harold Durfee (2014) concluded about Austin, "the philosophy of the late J. L. Austin offered largely unrecognized foundations for a significant dialogue between linguistic analysis and phenomenology, which positions have been so deeply divided in contemporary thought."

We can and should so easily alter Austin's name to read, Colin Wilson, for he too, of course, was working away on exactly this knitting together of ostensibly divergent patterns of philosophy—the so-called Analytic British and the supposedly less prescriptive Continental. I have already mentioned, of course, that Wilson connated his own version of Existentialism, by drawing from an European initiative and overlaying it with an English analytical optimism.

Indeed the two poles are not as far apart, as Wilson himself stressed in 1965, when he coupled Husserl and Wittgenstein as both essentially labouring over the same approach, and that both, "suggested what was wrong: the [language] drill was made of base metal" (*Beyond the Outsider*).

The essential difference here is that Wilson stood firm building on a united philosophy, while both Husserl and Wittgenstein somewhat undermined the foundations, by not reconciling the two routes into a superhighway. By this statement, I mean that while British Analytic philosophy dove headfirst into the minutiae of words to the extent of abnegating a corresponding 'world', Continental philosophy swam from the phenomenology of Husserl, which promised the 'world' would be revealed by an extensive *epoché* process, but later submerged somewhat into Saussurean Structuralism and the concomitant Post-structuralism of Derrida. In other words, Husserl was abnegated, or at best misconstrued by his continental peers and Wittgenstein was adopted more so by the analytic band of Englishmen—much to his apparent discomfit. There was, then, no cohesion whatsoever, until Wilson's holistic *oeuvre* provided the glue recombining both avenues, which were never that far apart to begin with.

Indeed as Roche (2013) points out, "The differences between the two schools may well be superficial features, and are certainly capable of being overstated so as to prevent a very misleading contrast."

In the end, then, Colin Wilson should now be accredited as an important harbinger of philosophical unification, along—perhaps—with J. L. Austin, given their approaches from different starting points and given the latter's somewhat underplayed hand in the deal. For both are positing, and in Wilson's case actually attempting to construct high above, a clear and completely united philosophical highway for all to travel along.

This leads to my fourth incremental statement regarding Wilson's importance as a philosopher. In such a way, Wilson is so far outside that he is back inside the pantheon of philosophy, as a philosophical alchemist—an aspect of his writings that perhaps has been overlooked, in the more recent clamour to read his imaginative fiction and his perambulations into criminality and occult side-roads. More than being the existentialist outsider philosopher then, Wilson, for all his synthesizing, is also an important analytical thinker whose works on language deserve far more intensive discussion and discovery, given they are integral to his *Weltanschauung* and not separable.

Ultimately, he cannot be described as solely an English/British philosopher or as a Continental savant either, for he is both at the same time. I firmly believe that he would concur with this assertion. I also remember reading across several books by and about Wilson, the anecdote he writes about Iris Murdoch, who wanted to send him to university. "She thought quite wrongly that what I needed was to train my mind," says Wilson. "Obviously far from making me write better books, it would have crippled me" (Theroux, 2002). Perhaps so, but this recollection leads me to assert that many universities should now be including Wilson as an integral part of their philosophy courses.

References

Anonymous (1967). Review of : *Introduction to the New Existentialism. Times Literary Supplement*, January 15.

Appignanesi, Richard (2002). 'Richard Appignanesi and Colin Wilson: Existentialism Today' www.iconbooks.co.uk/reviewart.cfm?ArticleID=23 Accessed June, 2003.

Bakewell, Sarah (2016). *At the Existentialist Café: Freedom, Being, and Apricot Cocktails.* London: Chatto and Windus.

Bassett, Maurice (1995). *Author's Emendations to 'The New Existentialism'.* California: Private publishing.

Benson, Peter (2014). 'Derrida on Language'. *Philosophy Now* Issue100, January/February.

Bertonneau, Thomas (2011). 'Fighting Against Sleep:

Necessary Doubt as a Phenomenological Thriller' in Colin Stanley (Ed.) *Around the Outsider: Essays Presented to Colin Wilson on the Occasion of His 80th birthday* Alresford: John Hunt Publishing.

Bertonneau, Thomas (2016). 'Anything but Bland Conformity', a review of Colin Stanley (Ed.) Colin Wilson: *Collected Essays on Philosophers.* http://www.kirkcenter.org/bookman/article/anything-but-bland-conformity Accessed November, 2016.

Bolea, Stefan Ion (undated). *The Existential Philosophical Approach: Basic Concepts* Unpublished Ph.D thesis, Romania. http://doctorat.ubbcluj.ro/sustinerea_publica/rezumate/20 12/filosofie/Bolea_Tit_Stefan_EN.pdf Accessed June, 2015.

Collini, Stefan (2006). *Absent Minds: Intellectuals in Britain* Oxford: OUP.

Coniam, Matthew (2001). 'The Forgotten Existentialist' *Philosophy Now*, Issue 32, June/July.

Crowell, Steven (Ed.) (2012). *The Cambridge Companion to Existentialism* Cambridge: Cambridge University Press.

Dossor, Howard (1996) in Colin Stanley (Ed.). *The Philosophy of Colin Wilson: Three perspectives.* Nottingham: Paupers' Press.

Durfee, Harold (2014). 'Austin and Phenomenology'. *Journal of the British Society for Phenomenology*, Volume 2, 1971, Issue 3, pp. 170-176.

Grayling, A. C., Goulder, Naomi and Pyle, Andrew (Eds.) (2006). *The Continuum Encyclopaedia of British Philosophy* London: Thoemmes.

Gier, Nicholas F. (2007). 'Wittgenstein and Deconstruction'. *Review of Contemporary Philosophy* No.6.

http://www.webpages.uidaho.edu/ngier/WittDeCon.htm Accessed March, 2018.

Green, Paul (2004.) '*Dreaming to Some Purpose* the autobiography of Colin Wilson' http://www.culturecourt.com/Br.Paul/lit/ColinWilson.htm Accessed October 2004.

Griffiths, Neil (2007). 'Neil Griffiths Top Ten Books About Outsiders' http://www.theguardian.com/books/2007/jul/04/top10s.outsiders Accessed February, 2015.

Howarth-Williams, Martin (1977). *R. D. Laing: His Work and its Relevance for Sociology*. London: Routledge.

Lachmann, Gary (2016). *Beyond the Robot, The Life and Work of Colin Wilson*. New York: TarcherPerigee.

Listik, Yonathan (2015). 'Derrida's Performance'. *Philosophy Now* Issue.107, November.

Magee, Brian (1971). *Modern British Philosophy*. Oxford: OUP.

Marshall, James D. (2004). 'Two Forms of Philosophical Argument or Critique'. *Educational Philosophy and Theory*, Vol. 36, No. 4, pp. 459-469.

Marshall, James D. (2006). 'Philosophy, Polemics, Education'. *Studies in Philosophy and Education*, Vol. 26, No. 2, pp. 97-109.

Moorhouse, John (1998) in Colin Stanley (Ed.). *Colin Wilson, Two Essays: 'The English Existentialist' and 'Spiders and Outsiders'* (Colin Wilson Studies, no. 1). Nottingham: Paupers' Press.

Montgomery, Michael R. (2016). 'Radical Existentialism *The Outsider*'. Presentation, Society for Existential Analysis Annual Conference, October 1.

Ree, Martin (1993). 'English Philosophy in the Fifties' *Radical Philosophy* 65, Autumn.

Roche, Maurice (2013). *Phenomenology, Language and the Social Sciences* London: Routledge.
Rycroft, John (2010). *Swinging City: A Cultural Geography of London 1950–1974* Surrey: Ashgate.
Schofield, Harry (2013). *The Philosophy of Education: An Introduction* London: Routledge.
Shand, John (1996) in Colin Stanley (Ed.) *'Colin Wilson as Philosopher' & 'Faculty X, Consciousness and the Transcendence of Time'*. Nottingham: Paupers' Press.
Shand, John (2004.) 'Colin Wilson: The Joyful Philosopher'. https://www.academia.edu/183641/Colin_Wilson_Thought_Against_Defeat Accessed June, 2014.
Shand, John (2005). Review of *Existentialism* edited by Robert C. Solomon.. *Philosophy Now*, Issue. 53, November-December.
Shand, John (2016) 'Introduction', in Stanley, Colin (Ed) (2016). Colin Wilson *Collected Essays on Philosophers*. Newcastle: Cambridge Scholars Publishing.
Solomon, Robert (2004). *Existentialism* Oxford: OUP.
Spurgeon, Brad (2006). *Colin Wilson: Philosopher of Optimism* Manchester: Michael Butterworth Books.
Stanley, Colin (Ed) (2016). Colin Wilson *Collected Essays on Philosophers*. Newcastle: Cambridge Scholars Publishing.
Theroux, Louis (2002). 'In conversation with Colin Wilson'. *The Idler*—'The Love Issue' 30, Summer, pp. 80-99.
Wilson, Colin (1957). *Religion and the Rebel*. London: Victor Gollancz.
Wilson, Colin (1962). *The Strength to Dream*. London: Victor Gollancz.
Wilson, Colin (1965). *Beyond the Outsider*. London: Pan Books.
Wilson, Colin (1966). *Introduction to the New Existentialism*.

London: Hutchinson.

Wilson, Colin (1967) *The New Analytic Philosophy*. Big Sur, CA: Esalen Institute Recordings.

Wilson, Colin (1968). 'What is a Philosopher? The Thinkers'. *The Daily Telegraph Magazine* Number 213, November.

Wilson, Colin (1969). *The Philosophers Stone*. London: Barker.

Wilson, Colin (1969). *Voyage to a Beginning: a preliminary autobiography*. London: Cecil and Amelia Woolf.

Wilson, Colin (1972). *New Pathways in Psychology: Maslow and the Post-Freudian Revolution*. London: Victor Gollancz.

Wilson, Colin (1980). *The New Existentialism*. London: Wildwood House.

Wilson, Colin (1988). *Essay on the New Existentialism*. Nottingham: Paupers' Press.

Wilson, Colin (1998). *Below the Iceberg, Anti-Sartre and other essays*. San Bernadino: Borgo Press.

Wilson, Colin (1998). 'Notes on Derrida for Rowan', in *Below the Iceberg, Anti-Sartre and other essays*. San Bernadino: Borgo Press.

Wilson, Colin (1998). 'Below the Iceberg', in *Below the Iceberg, Anti-Sartre and other essays*. San Bernadino: Borgo Press.

Wilson, Colin (2010). 'An Essay on *Introduction to the New Existentialism*'.
http://web.mac.com/philco1/iWeb/Colin%20Wilson/Essays%20by%20Colin.html
Accessed June, 2010.

Woessner, Martin (2012). 'Angst Across the Channel', in

More than the Existentialist Outsider

Robert Bernasconi and Jonathan Judaken (Eds) *Situating Existentialism: Key Texts in Context*. New York: Colombia University Press.

Personal statement:
I have written extensively about Wilson's New Existentialism and have sometimes also critiqued rather widely, several aspects of his philosophy, which he also instinctively and determinedly promulgated in whatever he wrote, be it fiction or non-fiction. I did not here enumerate these criticisms of the form and content inherent in some of his work, several of which I have indeed been an agent of. Let me term this deliberate omission, an *epoché*.

Indeed, I have also frequently noted that I would bracket out these—to me—valid criticisms and concentrate on what he was trying to say. At the same time attesting to his uniqueness, even on a field where outsiders played freely; namely by his being an existentialist outsider, but well and truly beyond even this designation, most especially because he continued to embrace some of the prime tenets of an 'insider' analytical qua (British) Language Philosophy in an overall philosophical synthesis.

I also refer those interested to these articles and books written by me accordingly (see below):

Rapatahana, Vaughan (2011). 'Colin Wilson as Hydra'. *Philosophy Now* 85 July-August.
Rapatahana, Vaughan (2014). 'Colin Wilson (1931-2013) Obituary'. *Philosophy Now* 101, March-April.
Rapatahana, Vaughan (2016). 'Brief Lives: Colin Wilson'. *Philosophy Now* 112 February-March.

https://philosophynow.org/issues/112/Colin_Wilson_1931 -2013

Rapatahana, Vaughan (2017). Review of *Colin Wilson on Philosophers* edited Colin Stanley. *Philosophy Now* 119 April-May.

Rapatahana, Vaughan (2017). 'Colin Wilson as Existentialist Outsider' in Colin Stanley (Ed). *Proceedings of the First International Colin Wilson Conference.* Newcastle: Cambridge Scholars Publishing.

Rapatahana, Vaughan (2012). *Philosophical (a)Musings.* USA: Entropy Press.

Rapatahana, Vaughan (2001). *Colin Wilson as Mystic.* Nottingham: Paupers' Press.

Rapatahana, Vaughan (1995). *Existential Literary Criticism and the Novels of Colin Wilson.* Ph.D thesis, University of Auckland, New Zealand.

NB. I also wrote for *Abraxas*, in several issues, and online in several websites pertaining to Colin Wilson.

Finally, readers might be interested in two further books I instigated, which concern the viability of English as being utilized as a world language for philosophy:

Rapatahana, Vaughan and Bunce, Pauline (2012). *English Language as Hydra.* Bristol: Multilingual Matters.

Bunce, Pauline; Phillipson, Robert; Rapatahana, Vaughan; Tupas, Ruanni (2016). *Why English? Confronting the Hydra.* Bristol: Multilingual Matters.

Colin Wilson Studies:

Books on the life and work of Colin Wilson written by experts and scholars worldwide.

ISSN: 0959-180-X. Series Editor: Colin Stanley.

#1. MOORHOUSE, John and NEWMAN, Paul: *Colin Wilson, two essays: 'The English Existentialist' and 'Spiders and Outsiders' (including an interview with the author.)* £5.95. Paper. 50p. 0-946650-11-X.

#2. STANLEY, Colin: *'The Nature of Freedom' and other essays.* £5.95/ £16.95. Paper/Hardback. 33p. 0-946650-17-9 Paper/ 27-6. Hard.

#3. TROWELL, Michael: *Colin Wilson, the positive approach: a response to a critic.* £5.95/£16.95. Paper/Hard. 36p. 0-946650-25-X .Paper/ 26-8. Hard.

#4. SMALLDON, Jeffrey: *Human Nature Stained: Colin Wilson and the existential study of modem murder.* £5.95/£16.95. Paper/Hard. 38p. 0-946650-28-4. Paper

#6. LACHMAN, Gary: *Two essays on Colin Wilson: World Rejection and Criminal Romantics & From Outsider to Post-Tragic Man.* £8.95. Paper. 94p. 0-946650-52-7 *

#7. NEWMAN, Paul: *Murder as an Antidote for Boredom: the novels of Laura Del Rivo, Colin Wilson and Bill Hopkins.* £8.95. Paper. 74p. 0-946650-57-8.

#8. SHAND, John and LACHMAN, Gary: *Colin Wilson as Philosopher and Faculty X, Consciousness and the Transcendence of Time.* £6.95. Paper. 35p. 0-946650-59-4.

#9. DOSSOR, Howard: *The Philosophy of Colin Wilson.* £6.95.Paper. 42p.0-946650-58-6.

#11. ROBERTSON, Vaughan: *Wilson as Mystic.* £8.95. Paper. 83p. 0-946650-74-8.

#12. GREENWELL, Tom: *Chepstow Road: a literary comedy in two acts.* £9.95. Paper. xii, 120p. 0-946650-78-0.

#15. STANLEY, Colin: *Colin Wilson's Outsider Cycle: a guide for students.* £7.95. Paper. iv, 158p. 9780946650965.*

#16. WILSON, Colin: *Existential Criticism: selected book reviews* [Edited by Colin Stanley] £14.95. Paper. iv, 283p. 9780946650989. Limited edition of 100.

#18. DILLER, Antoni: *Stuart Holroyd: Years of Anger and Beyond.* £7.95. Paper. 56p. 9780946650149.

#19. CAMPION, Sidney R. *The Sound Barrier: a study of the ideas of Colin Wilson.* £12.95. Paper. iv, 194p. 9780946650811. Limited edition of 100 numbered copies.*

#20/1 DALY, Adam: *The Outsider-Writer, volume 1.* £16.95. Paper, 394p. 9780956866301

#20/2 DALY, Adam: *The Outsider-Writer, volume 2.* £16.95. Paper. 345p. 9780956866318

#21. WILSON, Colin: *Comments on Boredom* and *Evolutionary Humanism and the New Psychology.* £7.95. Paper. 50p. 9780956866325. *

#22 WILSON, Colin: *Introduction to* The Faces of Evil: *an unpublished book.* £8.95. Paper. 76p., 9780956866332. *

#23 STANLEY, Colin: *Colin Wilson's Existential Literary Criticism: a guide for students.* £12.95. Paper. 201p. 9780956866349.*

#25 TREDELL, Nicolas: *Novels to Some Purpose.* £17.95. Paper. 554p. 9780956866363.*

#26 STANLEY, Colin (ed) *The Writing of* Adrift in Soho *including Charles Russell's* The Other Side of Town. £7.95. Paper. 88p. 9780956866370 *

#27 WILSON, Colin: *Colin Wilson's* 'Lulu': *an unfinished novel.* £9.95. Paper. 184p. 9780956866387. *

#28 COULTHARD, Philip: *Lurker at the Indifference Threshold.* £7.95. Paper. 111p. 9780995597822

*Also available as a Kindle book
All quoted prices subject to alteration

**Paupers' Press, 37 Quayside Close, Nottingham NG2 3BP
United Kingdom
www.pauperspress.co.uk**

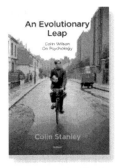

AN EVOLUTIONARY LEAP
Colin Wilson On Psychology

BY COLIN STANLEY

Price:	£ 17.99/$ 29.95
Pbk	144pp, September 2016
ISBN:	9781782204442

BIC Code: Psychology (JM)

When the existential philosopher Colin Wilson died in December 2013, it was suggested by one perceptive obituary writer that, despite the seemingly diverse subject matter of his books, his true legacy lay in the field of Consciousness Studies. This is particularly apparent when studying his many essays and books on psychology and taking into consideration his close association with the celebrated American psychologist Abraham Maslow whose concept of 'Peak Experiences'(PEs) became, for Wilson, an important link to experiencing enhanced consciousness. Maslow, however, felt that PEs could not be induced at will; Wilson thought otherwise and through his work sought to encourage his readers and students to live more vital and appreciative lives thereby paving the way toward an evolutionary leap for mankind in consciousness—indeed, a change in consciousness that would potentially change everything.

In this study, Colin Stanley, Wilson's bibliographer and author of Colin Wilson's 'Outsider Cycle': A Guide for Students and Colin Wilson's 'Occult Trilogy': A Guide for Students, provides an illuminating essay on each of Wilson's nine major books on psychology. Also included is Wilson's 'Notes on Psychology' to the psychiatrist George Pransky and 'Remembering the Outsider', Stanley's Colin Wilson obituary.

'It is to Colin Stanley's great credit that he has here not only compiled and commented on many of Wilson's most significant writings on psychology, but also done so in such a cogent fashion. This book, then, is essential reading for anyone with even a modicum of interest in human evolution.'
—Dr Vaughan Rapatahana, author of Wilson as Mystic

Contents

- The Age of Defeat (1959)
- Origins of the Sexual Impulse (1963)
- New Pathways in Psychology: Maslow and the Post-Freudian Revolution (1972)
- Frankenstein's Castle: The Right Brain—Door to Wisdom (1980)
- The Quest for Wilhelm Reich (1981)
- Access to Inner Worlds: The Story of Brad Absetz (1983)
- Lord of the Underworld: Jung and the Twentieth Century (1984/1988)
- The Misfits: A Study of Sexual Outsiders (1988)
- Super Consciousness: The Quest for the Peak Experience (2007/2009)

About the Authors

COLIN STANLEY is the editor of Colin Wilson Studies, a series of books and extended essays, written by Wilson scholars worldwide. He is the managing editor of Paupers' Press, and works part-time for Nottingham Trent University.

COLIN WILSON (1931-2013) was a writer and philosopher who came to prominence with the success of his first book The Outsider (1956). Essentially an existential philosopher, he has also written on crime, psychology, sex, the occult, literature, music, unexplained phenomena, history, and over twenty novels in various genres.

WWW.KARNACBOOKS.COM